The Taking of the Stone of Destiny

THE TAKING OF THE STONE OF DESTINY

Ian R Hamilton QC

LOCHAR PUBLISHING · MOFFAT · SCOTLAND

© Ian Hamilton 1991
Published by Lochar Publishing Limited
MOFFAT DG10 9ED

British Library Cataloguing in Publication Data

Hamilton, Ian
The Taking of the Stone of Destiny.
I. Title
942.132

ISBN 0-948403-24-1

Typeset in 11pt on 13pt Palatino by Origination,
Dunstable, Beds., and printed by Harper Collins
Manufacturing, Glasgow.

Chapter One

I am a Queen's Counsel in a state of treason against Westminster. Yet for many years I was ashamed of this book. Never of our action; only of the book. It was first published when I was a stripling of twenty-five, and knew how to put the world to rights. Striplings should not write books, or so I thought. They put things on record which cling to the author in after years. I long hung my head in shame at the brashness of the youth who wrote these pages. Worse. When I was doing other interesting things I disliked being referred to as 'The Stone Man'. I still do. For nearly forty years I refused to read what I had written here.

Now I know I was wrong. Not wrong in what I wrote, but wrong to be ashamed of it. This is a youngster's book, and I was immeasurably lucky to be that youngster. I am now a member of the establishment, not of that old, worn out, Anglicised establishment of second raters, but of the new one, which proudly affirms the ancient doctrine of our law that the power of government resides with the Scottish people, and not at Westminster. I look back on my visit to that other Westminster without dismay or shame, but with a great elation. I done it. Me and some others. That girl and those boys done well. I was one of them. It was a great adventure.

I have had many other adventures since. Yet this was the first and most important one. It set the tone for my whole life. It taught me that non-conformity in thought and deed is the only vital life. The individual is more important than the mass. Any single person can change history. MPs are the least effectual of citizens. Political parties are for sheep-minds. Heresy is Godliness. And so on. It was the first major event in a life in which I have loved greatly, and in which I have been both loved and hated in return. I would never have it otherwise. To inspire only respect is to fail. Respect is a form of indifference.

I have therefore not changed much in a book which was first

published in 1952. I have added two chapters at the end to bring the story up to date, but the story itself remains the same. The extravagances of youth are all there. I hereby homologate and accept them. Every single word and extravagance.

Yet in accepting them I have one qualification to make. As a youngster I was far too moderate. Away with English government, in every aspect. That is now my view. English government is for the English, and I am a Scot. Not a Scottish Nationalist. I do not need any such desperate description to define my love for my country. Indeed, I think that nationalism can be dangerously akin to racialism, and to be a racialist is to defy the common humanity of all mankind. I am a simple Scot, and I want my country to take its place in Europe and in the world. We Scots are European, not English, not British. In the muddled way of youth I set out to make these views public not by speech or writing, but by action.

Most, but not all, of the action takes place in an Abbey. This might be described as the desecration of altars, something the English have been quick to point out, although it was they who burned our fine Border Abbeys. I am now an agnostic, and I was once a Presbyterian. Presbyterians know no altars, but I respect their veneration in others. I remind my Roman Catholic friends that Westminster Abbey is in the hands of the Anglican heresy. Roman Catholics should not therefore be offended by our actions. As for Anglicans themselves. Hmmmmm! When you use your churches to reset stolen property you've got it coming to you. This story is about how it came to you.

But the story of the Stone of Destiny should tell itself. This is it.

Forty years on.
I have rewritten the next two chapters. In the 1952 edition they were political propaganda of the most shameless kind. There is now not a word of political propaganda in any of this book. I am a mendacious liar if that is not true. Read on and find out.

Chapter Two

The Stone of Destiny had always been in my mind as a symbol of the continued existence of the Scottish nation. How I first learned about it is a strange story. Cranks, eccentrics, and like subversives might well be encouraged by this story. These are the people who can only hope to cause ripples on the smooth surface of any society, but ripples on a pool can reach a far shore. That far and unlikely shore was our four-room semi-detached house in a Paisley suburb. I was born in one of the rooms of that house, and I grew up in it.

To that house came every day except Sunday two newspapers. One was called the *Bulletin*, and the other the *Glasgow Herald*. The *Bulletin* was the sister paper of the *Herald*, and it was directed at the sisters and wives of the *Herald* readership, so my mother read it. I was a child, newly able to read, and there were many pictures in it. What with looking at the pictures, and spelling out the text I developed an interest in the *Bulletin*. It was edited by a secret and private Scottish patriot called J.M. Reid. He did what he could in his quiet way to keep his readers informed of Scotland, and of Scottish history.

History is written by the usurpers. To this day, therefore, little is known by the ordinary Scot about our country's history. Its teaching is quietly discouraged. Once it was more than quietly discouraged. It was suppressed. Any time England invaded Scotland, the invaders sought out every scrap of paper which contained the records of our country and, when they were driven back, took them south, wiping their bloody noses on our parchments. Nevertheless some of these records survived, even if they were kept in London.

To London, with their hats off, and meek words in their mouths, went some Scottish historians in the 1930s. 'Please,' they said, 'could we have some of our records back?' and, because for many years things had been quiet in Scotland, London relented. Some

9

of the records were returned. I am not quite sure what they were. I think they were mediaeval Treasury Accounts. Whatever they were, their generous return caused a flutter of interest. We were beginning to have a history again. This is where the eccentrics and subversives come in.

Wendy Wood was one of these eccentrics. She lived her life for Scotland, and often paraded the streets as a walking bill-board announcing her views. When the Treasury Records came back, she paraded in the Royal Mile with a sandwich board, and she was photographed. The sandwich board read ENGLAND DISGORGES SOME OF THE LOOT, BUT WHERE IS THE STONE OF DESTINY? J.M. Reid printed that photograph in the Bulletin, and I remember the big black scrawly writing to this day. I was a small boy when I saw it and I asked my mother about it.

Mothers are difficult when it comes to stamping out a nation's history. Mothers have a race memory. My own mother never read a history book in her life, yet she had a fund of stories, and from the time I was too old to be crooned over, the stories she told were of the old Scottish folk heroes. These stories must have been passed down to her from her own mother, and so back to the roots of time. For that simple woman, history had passed into legend, and she told me these legends. I was familiar with that sallow, smiling, thoughtful throat-slitter, the Good Lord James, before I could read, and Black Agnes of Dunbar seemed like some relative, not all that long dead. I can still picture her, with her black wind-blown hair and her sparkling dark eyes as she drove the English off by waving a contemptuous duster at them from her castle walls. The old Scotland lives on in many a mother's memory. To my mother, then, I took this picture of Wendy Wood, and demanded an explanation. What was the Stone of Destiny?

She told me the story. When my brother and I fenced with our toy swords, we fought between us as to who should be Wallace, and who should be Bruce, so I understood what she said. The

10

story she told fitted into my mind. I knew the background. I knew of the Wars of Independence. What I found difficult to understand was where London came in.

She told me how the Stone had been taken to London during these wars and never returned. She told me the older stories of how it had been brought to Argyll before the time of Saint Columba, and how since then every King of Scotland had been crowned sitting on it, until it was carried south during Edward I's invasion of 1296. 'And there have been among us one hundred and ten kings, and not one foreign born among them,' she said, quoting unconsciously and accurately from the Declaration of Arbroath of 1320.

'And why is it in London?' the child asked.

And before it was brought to Scotland, the story went on, ignoring the question, the Scottish peoples had carried it with them as they migrated across Europe. All migrations take place westward, she said, and the Celtic peoples thought so much of the Stone that they carried it with them as the symbol of their nationality wherever they went.

'But why,' the question continued, 'is it in London, and not here among the Scots?'

She swerved round the question, obviously determined that I should know the whole story, and told me that it was supposed to be Jacob's pillow, on which he rested his head when he had the dream of the angels ascending and descending their heavenly ladder. And then she told me the ancient story from the Gaelic, in a rhyme which has remained ever with me,

> Unless the fates shall faithless prove,
> And prophets voice be vain.
> Where'er this sacred Stone is found,
> The Scottish race shall reign.

'But why...?' I continued.

And then she told me that when the English had been driven out, and the battles won, and the people's homes made secure, the English had promised to return the Stone, and had broken their promise.

A promise is sacred to a child; and a broken promise a terrible thing, long to be remembered. I remembered that broken promise all through my childhood. Something should be done to redress that old wrong.

I was little more than a child when war broke out in 1939. Yet it lasted long enough for me to grow into young manhood. I still had dreams of Scotland, and the dreams I dreamed were of a new Scotland, alive, full of ideas, and above all, full of self-confident young people unashamed of their birthright; not trying to be a sub species of the English, but being themselves. I dreamed of a people once more fulfilling its old role as the power-house of ideas for the world. We had done it before, and I knew we could do it again. I had many a tussle at school to assert these principles, and then one morning, after much heart-searching, I put these ideas into an attic of my mind, and went into a recruiting office and signed up. I wanted to be a fighter-pilot, and it seemed to me that this was a just war. I have never regretted the decision.

I was still a schoolboy and under age, but I was accepted for training as a pilot. Before I could be trained the war ended and my services as a pilot were no longer needed. Neverthless, I was detained for nearly three years in the Royal Air Force, servicing aeroplanes for other people to fly. It was a bitter, lonely time, but still the dream of Scotland persisted, and when I was demobilised in 1948, the dream was still with me. I enrolled at Glasgow University, but when I tried to formulate my thoughts and convert others, I found that everyone saw Scotland only in terms of Westminster Government, and what could be got from there. I wanted a Scotland which would reject Westminster utterly, but I could find no sympathisers, so I modified my ideas, and went along with the crowd. The welfare state was being created. I have never wavered in my support for the welfare state. A people who do not look after their disposessed is a race of savages. Yet the welfare state I saw being created was a cold chill thing, run by bureaucrats, adminstered from London. This was nothing like what the Scots could do by themselves. I was ashamed.

Shame was what characterised the mid twentieth century Scot. The shame was that we were not English. We had lost our sense of community. English customs, English pronunciations, English table-manners, were the mark of success. You were nothing if you did not speak proper, and proper was to speak with a south of England accent, or as near to it as the inherited muscles of the Scottish lips and tongue could manage. People even tried to think as the English did, and if there is one thing a people cannot do, it is to use the thought processes of another people. Most Scots thought of themselves as a sort of second class English.

Well. I didn't. Screw them. I would show them. Fellow Scots and English as well, I would show them. I would show the world, for that matter. There was no enmity towards the English in this and no hatred. I have never hated the English, although I have frequently pitied them. A people who have so frequently been conquered is to be pitied, but that is another matter. They have this saving grace, however, when they come to live among us. They train easily and civilise very quickly, most of them anyway. But gang warily when you get under an Englishman's skin. Before you get very deep you reach a thick layer of woad.

I had no intention in these days of ganging warily. I tripped when I tried. I still do. The only place where I can open my mouth without once again ruining my career is in the dentist's chair. In 1950, though, I was lucky enough to meet a man after my own heart, who helped to canalise my thoughts, and who set my mind to work in a more practical fashion. He was John MacDonald MacCormick, Lord Rector of Glasgow University, an honorary office. Election to it is by the student body. He was Chairman of the Scottish Covenant Association. The Scottish Covenant of 1948, which was promoted by him, had been signed by two million Scots. It asserted the right of Scotland to a Scottish Parliament for Scottish affairs. I went along with this. I took part. Yet my ambition went far beyond any reform in our political institutions. Scotland is only a small part of the earth's surface, and reform of our Government will be just another shuffle round of the people who hold power. It is reform in our attitude which is necessary. Whatever form of government we had, I wanted us to be a nation once again.

In the community of the world, nations are the individuals. Unless each nation makes its own separate and distinct contribution, humanity will fall into one amorphous mass, degenerate, indistinct, inactive. Variety is the ideal of nature, and we Scots were losing our distinctive variety. In the Scotland of the 1940s the official address was not Scotland but North Britain. Scotland was sleeping, and ignoring the great abilities which it had always possessed, and over which we had been put on sacred guard. The soul of a nation is in its people's keeping, and we no longer worried about our nation's soul. A person's soul is a trifle. A person who spends his life worrying about his salvation is not one I greatly admire. But a nation is a different thing. When we give away our soul, we have nothing left to give.

Now these are brave words, but as a young man I had the qualifications to utter them. My prime qualification was that I did not know my place. I never have. So many Scots, forgetting that one of the great features of our history is the mobility between the classes, have lapsed into the English habit of thought best expressed in the words, 'I wouldn't presume. I hope I know my place.' I always presume. I have never known my place. I am the second son of a tailor from Paisley, one of Scotland's provincial towns. Paisley will not easily forgive me for calling it that, for Paisley believes that it is the centre of the universe. Maybe it is. Certainly it was in Paisley, and in my father's house there that I first read Disraeli's great words, 'Learn to aspire.'

It was from my father that I also learned another lesson which has never left me, and which is this. Man is answerable only to God for his conduct, and if there is no God, a matter about which I have always been in great doubt, then he is answerable only to his own conscience. No man-made law tells a free man what to do. All it does is tell him what the punishments will be if he breaks the man-made law. It is the moral conscience of each individual which binds people together, and makes community life possible. Not courts, not lawyers, not judges, and certainly not the police. They are merely the regulators, but we are the people. It is we who make the community. Ourselves alone.

I was one of these people, and I was very much alone. In the autumn of 1949 I went down to London, and had my first look at the Stone of Destiny.

Chapter Three

My first reconnaissance of Westminster Abbey was a leisurely affair, and took in little detail. Detail would come later. I walked round, looked, and came back home satisfied that if I could get a few people together then it would all be possible, but I did not know a single person to turn to for help. It was a lonely time, and that was as far as it went that year. I knew John MacCormick only slightly then, and I had no close friends to confide in. I did indeed take my thoughts to Christopher Murray Grieve, the poet Hugh MacDiarmid, whose work I greatly admired, but the idea was to simmer with me for another year before it was to be formulated into any practical shape.

It is not easy for one young man on his own to formulate a plan of action. Dreams are for dreaming, and I did not regard myself as any sort of man of action. In a settled society ambitions are modest; day follows day, rubbing life thin, without any wear being noticed. The soldier who goes into action has a long training behind him, and is urged forward by the society he lives in. Ever present is the sanction of public opinion, forcing him to do things which would otherwise be forbidden. Nothing public urged me forward and indeed public opinion was very much against any sort of individual action. What I had in mind would put me outside the law, and I would have to face the consequences. In these circumstances the personal bar to action was very considerable. A cocoon of loneliness kept my dreams apart from reality.

Then in the autumn of 1950 I was invited to join the Glasgow student committee supporting John MacCormick's Rectorial candidature. I met all sorts of people through that and the cocoon began to wear thin. I met people who began to talk of strong measures, and who pointed to the melancholy history of Ireland. 'From the blood of martyrs,' they muttered, 'grow living nations.' Their eagerness to find a martyr was only paralleled by their desire to live to see the fruits of martyrdom. To be fair to them, most of them have lived to become martyrs to endless committee meetings in the Labour Party, or the Scottish National Party, so they are not to be laughed at. For my part, I would rather have the fire at the stake. Yet I listened to their talk.

Nowadays people sing rather than talk, but the old songs had not been revived then, and the new ones were unwritten. I listened silently to talk of sending Blue Bonnets over the Border, and wondered what it all meant. Of course it meant nothing, but I had not the self confidence to see that, and I felt that there was something missing in me. Did they know something that I didn't know? Were they going to do something that I couldn't do? Students have talked like this from time immemorial, but I did not know that then. I was over-awed by their terrible grown-up sophistication, but I enjoyed being a spectator at their performance. Blue Bonnets over the Border sounded great.

It was still a long way from listening to such talk, to crossing the Border on my own account. Clearly I needed a leader. I had not yet learned the lesson that there are no leaders worth following; that leaders are egocentric humbugs, who casually use others for their own ends. The way of a man with a maid is easily explained, but the way of a leader with those who follow him and think he is great, is one of the mysteries of life. Born leaders should be locked up. Leadership should be made a crime.

Yet the crime I contemplated needed a leader, and the crime itself fascinated me. Thoughts of it would not go away. It was, as I hear kids say in the slang of today, 'neat'. The Stone had been taken from Scotland to show that we had lost our liberty. Recovering it could be a pointer to our regaining it. A promise had been made by the Treaty of Northampton of 1328 that it would be returned, and that promise had never been kept. Why should fulfilment of that promise not be wrung from them by spiriting the Stone away at dead of night? It only weighed four or five hundredweight, which was not an impossible load for several men to carry. An empty chair speaks louder than a full house. Much louder than a full house if that House is a House of the

Westminster Parliament. It might just speak loud enough to awaken the people of Scotland.

For more than two thousand years the Stone had been the talisman of the Scottish people, and, for all I knew, they might still venerate it. My childhood memories came back to me and I remembered my mother's stories. I could almost see the thin smile on the long, lean, sallow face of my great hero, that slit-throat, the Good Lord James, the great guerilla leader of the Wars of Independence. Here was a guerilla operation in modern times, to be carried out, not by ambush, but by careful stealth in the enemy camp. The very audacity of the idea would have made him chuckle. It might have the same effect on the Scots of today. It was difficult; it could be spectacular; it was symbolic; it struck at the very heart of Englishry; it righted an ancient wrong; yet it hurt no one. Spiriting away four or five hundredweight of sacred Stone from the very heart of The Empire might fire the imagination of the world if it were carefully carried out. If we bungled it, we would be the only sufferers. But we must not bungle it. Who was to be the Good Lord James?

I found him on John MacCormick's Rectorial Committee. Among all the others he stood out as being the born leader of such an expedition. He was Bill Craig who was President of the Union that year, and a big man in the corporate life of the University. He had already graduated with one degree, and was studying for a further one. He had charm and ability, and above all he was able to lead. Indeed in the fun and frolic of a Rectorial election he led me into much temptation to which I readily succumbed, and together we got into all sorts of trouble, which was not real trouble, because he had the useful facility of knowing how not to be caught. I learned much from him.

He was twenty-six, a year older than I was, as I was just newly twenty-five. Like me he was small in stature, but he had a commanding presence. By sheer force of argument and personality he could persuade the most reluctant audience whether in public or private, because he was as able a speaker in debate as he was in committee. He was a ready-witted politician in the Liberal cause, which, then as now, permitted its adherents to formulate their own policy, and I don't mean that as a jibe.

For the job we contemplated, other qualities were needed than those of a politician, and he possessed these par excellence. Calm and unruffled in the most adverse of circumstances, he had that type of temperament which can never admit defeat, and will turn disaster into glorious victory. Add to that that he is small and Pictish, like so many Scots, because we are all as much Picts as Scots, and imagine a Puckish smile concealing a wicked sense of humour, and you have a picture of Bill.

Yet before I approached him I wanted to have something to lay before him. I dropped no more than a hint in the right quarter and saw from the reaction that there were people in Scotland not averse to financing such an enterprise. For my part the idea had now grown from a mere discontent to a passion that made me think of little else. Apart from the hint about finance I had mentioned the scheme to no one. The need for secrecy was great. I had seen others bluster and talk about what they were going to do, and then fail to get to the starting point, and I did not wish to be one of them.

My starting point came in early November of 1950. I knew then that my decision was made. I was going after the Stone. Hell mend you or bend you, I was going to have a crack at it. I became impatient of politics, and discussions and arguments, and closed my mind to them, for I was now convinced that my course of conduct was right, and if it was wrong, it hurt no one but myself. Further dreaming could not have made the issue clearer. I decided to approach Bill Craig.

I met him in the street one November afternoon, and prised him apart from his friends. I told him in a few words what was on my mind.

He laughed and swore at me when he heard what I had to say, and called me his evil genius. Here he was, on the threshold of his career, when I came along to tempt him from the path of success. I

19

was a fool, and the scheme was hair-brained and impossible, to say nothing of being illegal.

I reminded him of some of the things we had been up to recently, which had been on yon side of the law, and yet were still sweet to remember. There had been various misadventures including a Tory loud-speaker van that had been unaccountably silenced. He grinned.

'What are you going to do with it when you get it back to Scotland?' he asked.

'I haven't thought that far,' I said. 'We'll have to leave that to the people of Scotland. But it will at least show us whether or not they're worth fighting for. If they don't support us, then Scotland's as dead as Queen Anne.'

He thought for a long time, standing there in the street, as the light closed in on a grey November afternoon. It was in Sauchiehall Street, along near Charing Cross.

'All right,' he said at last. 'I'll come.'

I was rapturous. At last I had someone to whom I could pour out all my arguments, someone to whom I could tell how I thought it could be done. We walked together along the street towards the University, two little short men, their heads close together, the one small and dark and thin and intense, the other open faced and frank and laughing at my enthusiasms.

'It will shake the world,' I said. 'To raid the heart of London. To bring back the age old symbol of our country. A big stone gone and only an empty chair. Five pounds worth of stone. Two thousand years of history. Scotland will wake again.'

'You're a silly romantic,' he said. 'But I'll come.'

Forty years on.
That was how it began. From now on I go back to the original narrative, pretty much as it was written all those years ago.

Chapter Four

With Bill Craig in the operation, I was certain that our chances of success were greatly enhanced, and we settled down like a general staff to plan our campaign.

I do not think we were at all presumptuous in what we were trying to do. In the space of a few short hours we planned to show to the English Government that there was a limit to their domination of Scotland; we planned also to show to the world that Scotland was awake again, and above all we wished to give to the Scottish people a symbol of their liberty.

With our total ages little more than half the age of any single senior politician, we hoped to do something which might earn a place in the history books, and would almost certainly earn us an English jail-room. So what? It has been pointed out to me that many of the minor events which have gone to make Scottish history have been carried through by young men and women. It will be a bad day for any country when its young sit at home and do as their elders tell them. It will be even worse, and the end of all our freedoms, for the old as well as the young, when youngsters of conscience are afraid of the police.

From the beginning, we accepted that the police would inevitably catch up with us. Both Bill and myself were known as active supporters of the Covenant movement in Glasgow. Because there had been little illegal nationalist activity since before the war, we surmised that the police would have no dossiers of suspects to guide them. Police do not work by magic. When a crime is committed they look at the crime. Then they look at the modus operandi. Then they look at who's out of prison and draw up a list of suspects. For this crime there was a whole nation of suspects, or so we hoped. On the other hand, it seemed obvious to us that an exploit of this type could only be carried through by people with a great deal of free time on their hands. Such deduction on the part of the police would force them to suspect students, and since Glasgow University has always been a centre of Nationalist activity, we guessed that it would not be long before the police were on our tracks. There were then seven thousand students at Glasgow University, but we prided ourselves that we would be high on the list of suspects.

We were entirely mistaken in our assumption. We had always been led to believe that Scotland Yard, although perhaps slow, inexorably sifts every clue until it gets its man. It is rather disturbing to a law-abiding citizen like myself to discover that this is not the case. We sprinkled the Abbey with clues, yet Scotland Yard were clueless. So far from using induction and deduction, and all the scientific methods of criminal investigation, Scotland Yard seemed to lapse back into the days of the incantation and the bubbling pot. They conferred with a clairvoyant, who held his head in silence, and with a water-diviner who led them, presumably at public expense, to the River Trent. Up and down the country, in their search for the stone, water-diviners could be seen twitching twigs. Scotland Yard went daft.

Fortunately for the reputation of the British constabulary, things were different in Glasgow. While Scotland Yard was establishing its Department of Criminal Telepathy, Glasgow's Serious Crime squad, under Detective Inspector Kerr, was working quietly at the job he was paid to do. I have the most lively respect for Mr Kerr and his colleagues. As public officials they could have no sympathies, yet I know they must have hated their job. That did not matter; they had their duty to do and they did it efficiently. As far as I could ascertain, all the laurels on the side of the authorities must go to them. I have met the brains of Scotland Yard and was not impressed, but Inspector Kerr is a policeman with whom it is a privilege to have crossed swords.

Accepting the myth of the unbeatable police, we aimed not so much at success without discovery, but at success at all costs. Had we taken even elementary precautions, such as arranging alibis, laying down false clues, and ensuring that all who took part maintained complete silence, after the event as well as before, I do not think we would ever have been discovered. As it was, we accepted certain arrest; waited for the police to come; and it took them three months to find us.

Towards the middle of November I went along to Glasgow's Mitchell Library and withdrew all the books I could find which dealt with Westminster Abbey and the Stone of Destiny. I signed for these books in my own name, for if I had used a false one I might have been recognised, and the subject of my studies clearly revealed. In the face of arrest it seemed to matter little what name I used, although in the end the library slips with my name on them were the only concrete piece of evidence the police had against me.

I waded through pages of description and history, drew several maps, made calculations, and studied photographs. I followed all the guides step by step from the west door to the Battle of Britain Memorial. I found much that was of interest to me and a little that was of use to me. In the midst of my studies I was interrupted by a fellow student who, peering over my shoulder, was astounded at my choice of reading matter. I hastily explained that I was preparing a lecture that I was shortly to deliver to a church youth club. He accepted the explanation, although when the news broke at Christmas he must have thought it a thin one. To my knowledge he never mentioned the subject of my studies to anyone. He was a canny Scot who knew how to keep a quiet tongue in a time of seething interest.

Armed with the figures, maps and plans, and filled with the excitement of generalship, I approached another canny Scot, to see what money I could wheedle out of him. I knew that he was not a rich man, but I had every indication that he would beggar himself if it would prosper Scotland. The sum I had in mind was £50, quite a lot of money by my standards, and I suspect by his also. He was a Gael whose family came from Mull, and as I sat waiting to be shown into his office I reflected how often in either the major or the minor episodes of history it was the Gael who had helped the Lowlander, more than the Lowlander the Gael. It has always been thus. The Highlands and Islands are in material things the poorest part of our country, yet I could not think of any part of our history where they had not played their part, and ever a generous and noble one. So it was again. Although we had met on many occasions, he did not know me well. I would be just another youth to him. Now I was going to give him details to show that Bill and I could do something which had long been considered impossible. Rejection would have hurt me, and laughter at the idea might have left a permanent scar. I was shown into his little office. This was the first hurdle.

He was sitting behind his desk and he smiled and watched me as I came in. He was small of stature. with a high forehead and a narrow, deeply-lined face. His hair was rather untidy, but there was about him an air of shrewdness which I welcomed. I was in deadly earnest, and I felt that here was a man who would appreciate that, and not hum and scratch and talk about student pranks.

I sat down and told him what was in my mind. I launched out into the details and grew enthusiastic as I went into the possible results of the plan. He watched me intently. He was impressed. He asked me a few questions and I answered them. Then he asked, 'You appreciate the dangers and you know that you will probably go to jail?' I told him that I appreciated the dangers.

'You know,' he said, 'I was once in your position.' And he told me how in the early 'thirties there had been another plot to recover the Stone, and he had been in it. Unfortunately, one of his confederates had frustrated him by giving the details of the scheme to the Press.

He sat silent. I could see what was in his mind. He was full of enthusiasm, and desperately keen to help, but he felt that it was unfair to give us the money to run into danger while he sat safely in Glasgow.

'If you don't give us the money, I shall have to go to someone less reliable,' I said regretfully.

At that he laughed. 'I'll give you anything within reason,' he said.

'Can I have £10 now?' I asked. 'I'm leaving for London tonight.'

I was delighted. We were at last on the way to doing something which would not easily be forgotten. Conversation and argument were behind us. The decision had been made and there could be no regrets and no qualms. The bitter taste of procrastination was no longer in our mouths, for we were going forward.

A few hours later I caught the 10.30 p.m. train from Central Station. By a coincidence, Bill Craig was also going down to London that night as he was addressing a meeting in London University Union. Unfortunately, he was accompanied by another delegate from Glasgow University, so we could not travel together. We regretted this necessity, for we liked each other's company, but I did not wish anyone to know that I was in London. While I had innumerable reasons for a trip south I did not class myself as an accomplished liar, and I thought that the invention of a sick relative in London was a story which I could not readily sustain. Although the other student was of our own views, I did not wish to arouse his suspicions.

As I crossed the Border I was seized with shaking excitement. The Blue Bonnets were over the Border, and not for the first time. I thought of how my forefathers from Clydesdale had many times passed this way, in defence of the liberty of Scotland, or bent on hearty plunder. That had happened long ago, but the memory of old bitterness is not easily erased. And although I was travelling south with neither rape, nor arson, nor seige, nor pitched battle in my mind, but with only the recovery of a block of stone as my aim, I did not think, considering the times, that my forefathers would be ashamed of me.

When I reached London this excitement was redoubled. It was a fine sensation to be at the heart of England once again, but this time not as a serviceman on leave or as a tourist, or as a visitor, but as a spy, arranging something which, while it was not hostile to this mass of people, could hardly command their enthusiasm and support.

I was elated. At last I was doing instead of thinking. For years I had talked a little, and dreamed a little, and thought a little, and

25

read a little, and now as a result of my dreaming and thinking, I was at last on the threshold of action without which no young man is complete.

I went to a hotel near St. Pancras Station and registered in my own name, for I saw no reason for subterfuge. The hotel was clean enough and reasonably comfortable for its price, but full of that big city commercialism which aims at giving not a halfpenny more than a pound's service for twenty shillings.

It was afternoon, and as soon as I had washed and freshened up, I took the subway over to Westminster. The Abbey lay in a pale East Coast sunlight, rich and dignified and stately, like an Englishman's conception of his country's history. But when I saw the Houses of Parliament which lay behind it, I realised that it was a jewel set on a mud-bank.

I crossed Parliament Square and entered the dim sanctuary of the nave from the west door. It was quiet and peaceful. A handful of visitors lingered along the dim length of the building or moved respectfully round the grave of the Unknown Warrior. I joined the procession of sightseers, and for some considerable time moved about in the calm duskiness. It was, of course, not my first visit to the Abbey, and I had studied so many maps and plans that I already had a considerable knowledge of it. But I wanted to have a vivid picture of the whole building in my mind. In particular I wanted to learn all I could about locks and doors.

At length I came to the entrance to the eastern chapels, and was forced to pay my shilling entrance fee like a visitor to a common museum. Religion in England seems to be a lucrative trade, but I was more offended at the idea of a Scot being charged by an English cleric for permission to view the Stone of Destiny.

The Stone was contained in a box-like aperture under the seat of the Coronation Chair, which stood in Edward the Confessor's Chapel with its back to the rood-screen, which in turn acted as a back-drop to the high altar. I examined the Stone carefully. It is a block of rough-hewn sandstone twenty-six and three quarter inches long, by ten and three-quarter inches deep, by sixteen and three

26

quarter inches broad. These measurements came from a book. I did not measure it. I had not been able to find its weight, but we had reckoned that it would not be more than three hundred-weights, though we were later to discover to our cost that it was more than four. On either end a few links of chain terminating in an iron ring would provide handles which would be useful for carrying it.

The Chair itself provided no great difficulty. It is, I think, of oak and very ancient. It is indeed the oldest piece of furniture still used for the purpose for which it was made, which was to hold the Stone. A small lath along the front held the Stone in place, and I saw that this could easily be removed. I was anxious that we should be able to do this without damage, for I had a veneration for ancient workmanship. But if it needed to be jemmied away, jemmied it would be. The stolen Stone was behind it.

Having gorged myself on these details, I looked further afield. The corkscrew wooden stairs which led into the chapel would give considerable difficulty to two people dragging a heavy weight, and the iron grill through which I had passed when I paid my shilling might be locked at night. We might, however, be able to circumvent those difficulties by using the door which led through the rood-screen and past the high altar. I disliked thus invading what to some people was a holy place, but for my own part I had no dread of altars.

Before I left I engaged one of the guides in conversation. I was interested in the Abbey, very interested, but how did they keep it so clean? Surely an army of cleaners came on every night when the Abbey was closed. No? I made a mental note that we would not be likely to blunder into an army of cleaners. A few other leading questions and another prowl round showed me all there was to be seen. I was then able to leave the Abbey, taking with me all the information I required for successful burglary.

I collated this information in an adjacent pub. I had bought a guide-book which contained an excellent plan of the Abbey, and I spent my time filling in details which I had observed and wished to remember. It amused me to think that the Dean and Chapter were providing the drawing on which the plan of campaign was to be worked out. Thereafter, for the space of three hours, I wandered round the back streets between Victoria and Millbank, for I wanted a complete picture of all the approaches to the building. In the early evening I went back to my hotel and lay on the bed and smoked a cigarette. I had had little sleep the night before, and I had walked many hours that day on hard streets. In return I had a complete picture of the whole district. There was only one thing more I wanted to know, and that was what police activity there was in the vicinity of the Abbey in the hours of darkness.

I put out the light and slept. At eleven o'clock I rose and took a Tube to Westminster. My intention was to keep circling the Abbey all night making careful notes of all I saw. By one o'clock the streets were deserted, and only an occasional vehicle sped along the rear of the Abbey. I was particularly interested in Old Palace Yard. I continued my watching, making notes every quarter of an hour. As time passed, I became more and more satisfied, for only once did I see a policeman, and he was some distance from the building. The nearest one on permanent duty was three hundred yards away at the gateway to Palace Yard. At five o'clock I walked to Whitehall, hailed a taxi and returned to my hotel, well satisfied with my night's work.

Five hours later I was on the train for Glasgow. I was tired but full of burning contentment. I now knew beyond all shadow of doubt that what we planned was not beyond our capacity. The difficulty was there, but that was a challenge. From now on we were to face, not indecision, which is the most sick-making of all maladies, but only the cold recklessness of calculated risk-taking, which should make any youngster sing with joy.

Forty years on
These events took place before the days of terrorism, when there was still casualness rather than fear in the management of the affairs of state.

Youngsters were not the only naive ones. Although I had been taught to handle arms in the Forces there was no thought of going armed or indeed of using violence of any kind. Mahatma Gandhi was dead only two years, and he was then, and still is, one of my great heroes.

Another of my great heroes, although not perhaps in the international class of Mahatma Gandhi, was the man who financed us. I am pretty coy about his identity in this chapter. He was of course John MacDonald MacCormick, the founding father of the modern Home Rule movement. He was for years the closest of my friends. At that time, as the leader of the moderates, he could not be seen to be in any way associated with illegal acts. He was a great man, and I am glad that nowhere is there a statue to him, nor so far as I know even a portrait. Ikons for John are unneccessary. He is remembered in many hearts, not least my own, as a great, affectionate, humorous, dedicated human being, who taught me the fine lesson that high causes can be pursued without bitterness, and without too much solemnity either.

So far as the policemen who had to solve the puzzle are concerned, I later met many of them in court. But not as an accused. As an advocate, I cross-examined them for the defence, and later, as prosecuting Counsel, I examined them in chief for the Crown. Both sides loved the irony of it. There grew between us a mutual respect, amounting to affection. The only one I can still trace is Calum Robertson, now retired and living in Skye. Yon were great times, Calum. I'll throw away the cork in the bottle when we meet again.

Chapter Five

Four months after our raid on Westminster I was addressing a meeting in Aberdeen in support of Home Rule. Our Chairman was Professor Jones of Aberdeen University, who during the war had been one of the back-room boys of the War Ministry, and had been responsible for considerable advances in the technology of scientific warfare. His book, *Most Secret War*, is the classic work on the subject. I was interested to meet him, not only for himself and his erudition, but because he fascinated me as an academic who had parachuted into enemy held territory with the Commandos on raids on enemy scientific establishments. His job was to tell the soldiers which pieces of enemy equipment should be taken back home so that we could find out what the enemy was up to.

He still kept up with the Commando officers who had led these raids on the enemy. He assured me that they had a professional interest in our raid on the Abbey, quite apart from its political motive and its public repercussions. Theirs was the interest of the professional soldier in a coup which they felt fell within the province of their own profession. I had always been fascinated by the guerrilla nature of their operations, so like the traditional means of waging Scotland's wars, and I was flattered to find that they found some interest in our own.

Certainly in the days of preparation for the raid we tried to emulate what we believed to be their methods. There were a great many factors to be considered and allowed for, but while we had to admit that there was a great margin for chance, the more we planned and considered, the more many of these factors came under our control. Unlike the Commandos, however, our action was limited by political and humanitarian considerations. We had to succeed or come near to success, for if we failed miserably we would plunge ourselves, our movement, and our country into nation-wide derision, and as England was to learn to its cost, hearty laughter is a sharp weapon.

If it was planned as something of a military operation such

planning had its limits. The means at our disposal were slender. There was no one behind us for support. Unlike ordinary soldiers we were not expendable. The two of us were all there were. We had very little money, we had utterly put aside any question of using violence, for we desired a peaceful demonstration, and we were to work all the time in secret at the very centre of the enemy camp. But the greatest force working against us is one which no Commando ever knew. We were planning consciously to break laws which we had been trained from birth to revere and respect. For my part it was only the calm belief that a person's conscience is the ultimate law which kept me going.

Now that I had a clear idea of the geography of the place, our first and most obvious task was to find out exactly how much the Stone weighed. This was not as simple as might be imagined. All the books I had read on the subject had dealt with the Stone in fact and legend; one had even dealt with it as though it were a geological specimen. None, however, had given its weight and dimensions. Although we knew its approximate size, we did not wish to calculate its weight from the specific gravity of sandstone, lest an arithmetical blunder should throw us several hundredweights out. In this connection John MacCormick was able to help us. The next time I visited him I explained our trouble and he reached for his telephone.

'Bertie Gray's the man,' he said. 'He knows more about stone than anyone else in Scotland.'

He made an appointment for me, and I went along to visit Councillor Gray, who pursued the rather lugbrious trade of monumental sculptor. We met in his little office beside the Beresford Hotel in Sauchiehall Street, and I told him what was exciting me.

He was not surprised, for he had already had some inkling from our friend of what was afoot. I was delighted with his almost boyish desire to implicate himself art and part with us. Since he was Vice-Chairman of the Covenant Association, Rector's Assessor on Glasgow University Court, and a member of Glasgow Town Council, I should have stood in awe of him. Respect I undoubtedly had, but it was respect for the qualities which had sucked him into high office rather than for the high office itself. Awe I had none. Although he was as old as my father, he had a capacity for being as young as the company he kept. I numbered him among my closest friends. Much later in the story of the Stone he was to win my respect for the coolness with which he took risks. When the hunt was at its height, he it was who dodged the police, arranged for the repair of the Stone and acted as its chauffeur on many of its journeys about Scotland.

The Councillor did more than calculate the weight of the Stone for me. He got on the telephone to his mason's yard at Lambhill and gave some instructions. The next day he drove me out there, under the pretence that I was the prospective purchaser of the latest in tombstones. I casually admired some tombstones and slowly worked towards the corner of the yard which he indicated. There, among the long grass, lay a replica of the Stone of Destiny. It was twenty years old. It had been made in the late twenties in connection with another plot to recapture the Stone, a plot which had never come off. Lying on the ground it looked much bigger than I had imagined.

'It weighs four hundredweight,' he told me. An apprentice bearing a hammer approached, and I resumed my meditations among the tombstones and reflected that its weight was likely to be the cause of some strained muscles.

Following on my excursion to Lambhill, Bill, the Councillor, John MacCormick and myself met several times per week. During his visit to London, Bill had found time for a visit to Westminster, and his impressions tallied with mine. On the other hand, it was years since the other two had been there. They were able to act like a House of Lords with an impetuous Lower Chamber, and give us the benefit of minds which were not squinting from too much contemplation of the subject. As we talked, several salient points emerged.

In the first place, we decided that a daylight raid was out of the question. We regretted this decision, for it would have been a fine thing to have spirited away four hundredweight of stone in broad daylight from under the noses of the Dean and Chapter. But the difficulties were too great, and although we considered having a bath-chair made with a special aperture under the seat to contain the Stone, we realised that this would be of little use, since the Confessor's Chapel is up a flight of narrow wooden steps from the floor of the nave.

This meant that a night raid was essential, but before we moved to plan it, we came to the unanimous conclusion that the execution must be carried through by the smallest possible number of people. Scotland has no tradition of underground movements and secret societies, and the slightest hint of our intention meant ignominy and failure.

The last point which occupied our minds was what we should do with the Stone when we had removed it from the Abbey. We were certain that whatever else happened there would be a hue and cry up and down England, and every road on the Scottish Border would be watched. We therefore decided that we would take the Stone south, and hide it, to be recovered when the heat was off.

With all this in mind, we evolved the following plan. One of us would conceal himself in the Abbey towards closing time, and as soon as he had been locked in he would climb over the iron grill separating the east chapels from the nave and hide himself in the Confessor's Chapel which was then under repair. I claimed this honour for myself as the conception had been mine and I was selfish enough to demand as large a part as possible in its execution.

I would lie quietly in hiding, watching the night watchman and finding the pattern of his patrols, for although we knew that he came on duty at 6 p.m. and had an office some considerable distance from the Confessor's Chapel, we were not certain how often he patrolled the building.

At 2 a.m. or as soon thereafter as I was satisfied that the night watchman had completed his rounds, I was to screw the lock off the door leading from the Margaret Chapel to the Abbey grounds where an accomplice would be waiting. Failing that, I was to force the padlock from the door in Poets' Corner. The door from Poets' Corner and that from the Margaret Chapel are almost adjacent. We would then remove the Stone from the Chair, lash it to an iron bar, and carry it outside, where a small, inconspicuous car would be waiting. This car would drive to a quiet side-street where the Stone would be transferred to a larger and faster car which would head straight for Dartmoor, where the Stone would be hidden. Meanwhile the small car would race out towards Wales. If it had been seen outside the Abbey, and if the police recognised it and stopped it, the driver would try to convince the police that he had handed the Stone over to the Welsh Nationalists, whom, of course, we had not contacted and had no intention of contacting. This would lead to the police following up an entirely false scent in Wales, which might be useful when we returned to fetch the Stone from Dartmoor. This was a good plan. It was the basis of our subsequent action, but it had to be sorely amended under stress of circumstances, for the unforseeable always happens.

Having now arrived on the brink of action, Bill and I commenced to fix a date for the enterprise. To me, Christmas was the only possible time, for the English celebrate it in a very thorough way, and while we did not want to spoil their joys or tarnish their festival, I maintained that we should come down on them while they were lying in drink with their minds unbuttoned.

On the other hand Bill was in no mood for precipitate action. He had many engagements to fulfil over the Christmas and New Year period. In addition to the seasonal festivity the student body was preparing to celebrate the Fifth Centenary of the founding of the University, which event fell on 7 January 1951, and Bill, as President of the Union, was much in demand. He showed me his diary which contained inescapable engagements for every day over the Christmas and New Year period. The plan would keep, he argued. It could be done anytime. Some other factors might arise which would help us.

But I was not so sure. Secrets of this nature do not mature like good wine, and moreover I had screwed my resolution to the last turn, and I was not sure that it would not suddenly unwind if I was denied the prospect of immediate action. Bill was adamant. I was stubborn. It was the contest between the thruster, whose value is a sudden, furious output of power, followed by months of inertia, and the canny statesman who works and works and works, and can work and wait.

'I'll go myself,' I told him in the bitterness of my disappointment, and there the matter rested.

In the days that followed I was not a happy man. In my uneasiness, I almost lost sight of the final purpose and gave up the struggle; for I knew that if I did not go to Westminster that Christmas I would never go at any other time. There was no one else I could turn to in whom I could place the same confidence I had placed in Bill. He held a position of respect in the University, and many students, who would gladly have faced uneasy issues with him, would have turned away with a smile if I had asked them. Together we could have talked even a Scottish politician into helping us; alone, I knew of no one I could inspire.

Then as all the old arguments and plans came flooding back to me, I thought that there might still be a way. I remembered the £10 I had spent on my trip to London, and all the talk and thought and dreams about the Stone, and I decided that if I was not forever to consider myself a vain-mouthed braggart, I would have to go on, come what may.

At first I thought I might be able to design a little bogey on which I could place the Stone and wheel it from the Abbey like a baby in a pram. This baby weighed four hundredweight, and as I am only five foot six and weigh nine and a half stone, I was being madly optimistic. I had, however, a belief in my ability to lift a great weight if events proved it necessary, and when indeed the occasion arose, I did not find my strength lacking. What beat me in the end was the flight of wooden steps down which I would have to trundle the Stone from the Confessor's Chapel. Try as I would I could design no bogey which would silently descend stairs. It was the middle of December and I was back where I started.

Then, on the evening of December 15th, I attended the University's Daft Friday Dance which celebrates the end of the Martinmas Term. My partner was Kay Mathieson, a young teacher of Domestic Science, and a keen worker in the Scottish Covenant movement. I had met her two months previously at a party given by John MacCormick to celebrate the success of the Covenant plebiscite in the Scotstoun by-election.

Kay speaks with the quiet tongue that knows English only as a second language. She is small and dark and large eyed, and remote as a Hebridean island.

That night I was far from being a sociable companion. We sat in the bar having a quiet drink. Inwardly I moodily cursed Bill and sank deeper into that depression which comes when you have talked excitedly of great things and come back to a live present which contains only mediocre success, which in the long run is failure. My life was flavourless, and if I thought of anything, I was wondering if anyone, among the people I knew, would willingly throw over their future prospects and come to London.

Suddenly I knew without doubt.

Kay's political views were almost identical to mine. If anything, coming as she did from the ravaged Highlands, with their long memory of oppression and clearance, she was more extreme than I. She was, I was certain, an idealist who would not be greatly concerned about her own welfare if she could do anything to serve the good of her own people.

Above all she was discreet. In every movement there are small secrets, both social and political. The Scottish movement was no exception. I had known these secrets and kept them: other people had known them and kept or broken them. Kay had known them and although we had been together many times she had never mentioned them to me. I was certain that she was thoroughly reliable.

The advantages of having Kay with me came crowding in on me. A lovely woman is never suspect, and a brave woman could fire the imagination of the world. Kay could never hamper our plan; she could only assist it. Were we not planning something which would be meat and drink to the Sunday papers? Let us give it to them then, from the *hors d'oeuvre* to the brandy.

No chivalrous thoughts held me back even for a moment. While I was certain that no English court would punish Kay as rigorously as they would punish me, I knew that the results for her would not be pleasant. I knew that I was being unfair in exposing her to the cold and the minor hardship and the prison which would inevitable follow. I was certain, however, that Kay would catch the imagination of Scotland as her countrywoman, Flora MacDonald, had done in the Islands two centuries previously. Even if the operation failed, and the English imprisoned Kay, there would be such an explosion in Scotland as would rock Westminster to its venerable foundations. As for her as a person, she had to take the same risks as I was willing to take.

I had made my choice. I decided to put it to Kay and let her make hers.

I put down my drink and spoke to her for the first time in ten minutes. 'What are you doing at Christmas, Kay?'

'I'm going home,' she said.

'I'm going to London to bring back the Stone of Destiny.'

She laughed. 'I thought you had a hard head,' she said. 'You've only had one drink.'

'I mean it,' I said, and I did mean it. I looked at her and saw the smile fade from her face. Then she laughed again.

'So did Wendy Wood, and Compton MacKenzie and John MacCormick and Bertie Gray! Every Nationalist worth his salt has planned to get the Stone. Why do you think it's never been done before?'

'I don't know,' I said, and I still don't know. 'I can't understand why it's never been done, but I've been to London and I'm certain that we can do it.' I could see she was interested. 'Would you like to come?' I asked.

'No,' she said, and meant yes. 'What can I do?'

'You can drive,' I told her and outlined the plan.

'If we fail,' she said, 'We'll get shot out of the movement.'

I assured her that that would be the least of our worries.

I was delighted, for I knew she would come. I had lost one comrade and gained another, and as we danced that night I was for the first time certain of ultimate success. It was not a feeling springing out of any rational weighing of the odds against us. With Kay with us, as we were to find out, the odds were considerably shortened. In practical things women have practical minds, and if their feet are too often fixed to the ground, they are all the better placed for guiding men who have their heads in the clouds. On occasion when I have been inflated with impracticable ends and searching for possible means to meet them, I have had my nonsense, to say nothing of my vanity, pricked by the cold logic of a woman.

The recovery of the Stone was no exception. Throughout, Kay faced the cold and the excitement and the risk with a bland indifference. Time and again when things went wrong, and we descended into black depression, she kept her composure when we had nothing else left to cling to. The success of the whole episode probably owes more to sheer feminine practicality than anyone will ever know.

Forty years on.

I laughed immoderately as I typed up the last few paragraphs. The patronising of women has ever been one of man's great amusements, and I am surprised we have survived poisoning. 1950 was before the so-called liberation of women, and in these days we truly thought that they were fragile and inferior creatures. They seemed to like it, and expected to be treated in such a fashion, so in that fashion we treated them.

Women's Lib, which if I thought of it at all in 1950 I would have assumed stood for women's libido, has changed all that. The greatest advance (wo)mankind has made since the invention of the wheel has been the liberation of women, but that came after 1950. It would be wrong of me to re-write my attitudes in the light of subsequent changes.

In mitigation I plead that I too have changed with the times. Nowadays I work with women colleagues in the courts. I certainly don't think of them as fragile creatures, but I don't go the whole way with woman's equality. I am as equal to a woman advocate as I am to a hungry tigress.

The reference to the dangers and the cold need some explanation. At that time the main road to London was a thread strung with villages. It was narrow, winding, and not much used. It was not gritted for ice, and indeed many private car owners laid them up for the winter. Cars had no heaters, and winter motoring was still something of an adventure in itself. These were the reasons for my tenderness for Kay . . . . and yet, and yet. I suspect men will still go on being tender towards women, whether they like it or not. Ye canny shove yer granny aff a bus.

Chapter Six

The rapidity with which things happened after I approached Kay often fills me with astonishment. Within one week we had cut all our threads in Glasgow and taken the road south, with two compatriots, two cars and a sack full of house-breaking tools.

Before that was done, however, I felt that my first duty was to report the new addition to our forces to John MacCormick and Councillor Gray. I rang John MacCormick, and told him that I had found a friend to take on holiday with me. Although I had no reason to fear that his telephone was being tapped a natural canniness made me take care.

'Oh yes, Ian,' he said in his usual curt noncommittal way.

'I'm taking her for coffee. Could you meet us?'

There was a sudden hesitation in his voice as he heard that my associate was a woman. Then he named a place and time and hung up.

We were to meet that afternoon in Miss Rombach's restaurant in Waterloo Street. I passed the information on to Kay and made arrangements to meet her there. I arrived a few minutes late and found them already in conversation, for they were no strangers to each other. I sat down and we ordered coffee.

The older man took the initiative right away, and I was glad, for I was not used to diplomacy of this sort.

'Kay has been telling me that she wants to go for the Stone with you, Ian,' he said.

'I know,' I said. 'I think it's a very good idea.'

Kay sat quietly listening.

'Well, it would have its advantages,' he said, looking at Kay.

I knew from experience that I did not have to enumerate the advantages to this man. I had found, on many occasions before, that a word or a hint or a look could convey all that I could have said in ten sentences. A lesser man would have argued pro and argued con, and might even have doubted our morality to say nothing of our sanity. Not this man. He knew what we were after and saw the advantages in a flash.

'What do you think?' asked Kay, turning towards him and speaking for the first time.

'Well, you know, Kay,' he said. 'You'll lose your job as a teacher.'

'I know,' she said.

'And it's scarcely a task for a girl. Even the minor hardships of a trip to London by road at this time of the year are something you should consider.'

'I would be going home anyway,' she said; 'And there are no trains to Inverasdale.'

'One up for Kay,' I thought.

I sat back and listened to the conversation with a considerable amount of amusement. The man, proceeding carefully from point to point, opened up avenues of escape for Kay to run along had she been looking for an excuse to escape. The girl did not let her point drop for a moment and quietly parried all his objections.

At last it was Kay's chance to ask a question.

'Will I get expelled from the Covenant movement if I go?' she asked rather worriedly.

'Whatever else happens, they will not do that,' he said spiritedly, and thereafter Kay's decision to come with me was so unassailable that he desisted from badgering her.

We finished our coffee and rose to go. Outside it was a grey colourless evening. Wisps of starlings crossed the sky like swift smoke. We stood among the hurrying figures in Waterloo Street and John MacCormick looked at us and said quietly, 'For twenty years in the Scottish movement I've made it a rule never to ask anyone to do anything I wouldn't do myself. I can't help you any more with this, but if between now and Christmas you want to back out don't be frightened to come and tell me.'

We laughed at him, but as I went away I knew the bitterness of the mind torn two ways. This man had used himself ruthlessly in

41

the service of Scotland for half a lifetime. It had been his boast that he would use anyone as ruthlessly as he had used himself. Now, when his boast was being proved and someone else was going forward instead of himself, he found that it is easier to sacrifice oneself than one's friends.

The next day I approached one or two possible recruits. Three of them immediately turned me down for reasons the validity of which I was in no position to challenge. This disturbed me a great deal. For the first time there were people in possession of our intention who had no stake in the plan, and who were under no necessity to keep a still tongue. There was nothing I could do about this except trust to Scottish taciturnity, and in the months that followed my trust was justified.

The fourth man that I approached jumped at the opportunity with avid glee. He listened intently to the whole plan from beginning to end, and was as impatient to start as I was myself. Gavin Vernon, our number three, was a twenty-four year old engineering student who had the Scotsman's delight in the risky enterprise which aims at high things. He was quite short of stature, but heavily built and of considerable physical strength, which he delighted in showing. Opening beer-bottles with his teeth made him a useful man at a party. Although his features had the raw-boned, obstinate set usually associated with the Lowlander and were overset with a bristling English moustache he was far from dour. Indeed his mad recklessness got him into many scrapes that no dour Scot was designed for.

With three people our team was now complete and we were almost ready to leave. We met in my room in Park Quadrant and time and again went over our maps and diagrams. This was, I suppose, what the Royal Air Force calls briefing, and we briefed ourselves as often as we all had a spare moment to foregather. We were not trained to follow maps, and I was the only one with first-hand knowledge of the Abbey, so it was necessary for them to memorise every detail.

Meanwhile I had my own worries. I had collected a burglar's

tool-kit, including an immense jemmy of which I was inordinately proud. With loving care I had made a sling which left the jemmy hanging its twenty-four inches from my oxter to my trouser pocket. The only trouble was that when I bent down it was prone to slide from its sling. The files, wire, hacksaw, wrench etc, I carefully stowed about my person until I was fully equipped with the tools of my new profession. Then I would put on my coat, go down to the little cafe in Gibson Street and talk to my friends, with the delicious cold steel against me, and a private thin smile of sheer joy on my lips.

While I was running needless risks in cafes, Gavin was not idle. He had made arrangements to hire a car to take us to London. This would be the car we would use outside the Abbey, so it did not need to be particularly powerful. In London I had already arranged to hire the bigger car which we would need to transport the Stone to its hiding place on Dartmoor.

All this preparation was very costly, and I suddenly realised that our money was running out. I could not for the life of me approach our original benefactor, for £50 was more than I cared to take from him. I knew, however, who would be equally ready to help. I called again on Councillor Gray.

He was eager for news and greatly disturbed to hear that Kay was coming with us, for he seemed to feel a rough sort of responsibility for all the workers in the self-government movement. I quickly assured him that Kay had not been press-ganged, and thereafter, although his uneasiness grumbled away in his mind, it only occasionally erupted into complaint.

I left an uneasy Bertie who was suddenly poorer by £30. That was, I feel sure, of no consequence to him at the time, for he was the most generous of men. What was on his mind was our safety, and he would willingly have come with us to look after us had I not pointed out that the Vice-Chairman of the Covenant could never involve himself in illegality.

Having seen Bill and arranged a code to use if I had to telephone him from London, we were now ready to depart. That night,

Thursday, 21 December 1950, Gavin and Kay and I met to hold our last council before leaving. We parted early, for it would be the last full night's sleep we would have for many days.

The next morning I rose full of excitement, for this was to be the great day. It was cold and dismal, with a hint of raw frost, and although I knew that I had many miles to drive that night I was not dismayed. Nothing could stop us now. Not frost nor snow, nor the weather nor our plans, and not even ourselves because the decision had been made.

My mood of exultation was to some extent sullied by Gavin, however, for I discovered that instead of meeting me as arranged, he was still sleeping soundly in his bed. I went to his lodgings and had him out. Anger, friendship, and amazement that he could sleep while I was racked with excitement fought within me, but friendship won. The morning was ours and there was little cause for hurry.

Towards lunch-time we went down to the garage in Pitt Street and collected our hired car. We were rather disturbed when we saw it. It was an eight horse-power Ford and at least twelve years old. We could not find anything definitely wrong with it, and it was all we could afford. The engine pulled well, so we took it, but with a feeling of trepidation lest it should not stand up to the tests we were to put it to. Gavin went away to get used to it as he was to be driver-in-chief, and, having arranged to meet at 3 p.m., we parted, and I went home to pack my lovely tool-kit.

That afternoon at three o'clock I went to meet Gavin as arranged. To my dismay and impatience, when I got there he was talking to a tall, finely built young fellow, with a frank boyish face and a crop of golden hair. I hesitated on the street corner in an agony of anger. I had known that Gavin had told some of his friends where he was going, and I had accepted his assurances that that was the better way, since they would otherwise talk with loose and suspicious tongues. But it seemed madness to bring one of them to see us off.

When I had mastered my anger I went forward and was introduced to the newcomer. His name was Alan Stuart. His fine name and obvious honesty did not palliate my anger, and it was clear to me from the way Alan blushed that I had an ugly scowl on my face. Yet, like his namesake in *Kidnapped*, he was to prove the bonniest fighter I have ever met, bar only Kay Mathieson herself.

'I want to come with you,' said Alan, pleading rather than offering.

I thought quickly. I liked him instinctively, for he was boyish, unpretentious and unspoiled. But he was only twenty and looked younger, and I did not know how he would stand up if things went wrong. Furthermore, the plot had been laid for three people and it seemed unnecessary to take four. On the other hand, he knew all about us and could not gossip if he were with us.

'I'm sorry.' I said.

He could not have been more hurt if I had kicked him. 'It's all right,' he said through his disappointment. 'And the best of luck anyway.'

I warmed to him more. There was a simplicity in everything he said that erased my ill-temper, and chastised me for it.

'He could bring a car,' whispered Gavin.

'I could indeed,' said Alan eagerly as he caught the whisper.

My resistance fell, and I was naked against them.

'All right,' I said. 'You're on.'

His face lit up with boyish joy and he thanked me eagerly. He departed in a rush to arrange his affairs and get his car. He had gone twenty yards when he dashed back.

'Do you want an Armstrong or a Ford Anglia?' he asked.

'Would an Anglia carry four hundredweight?' I asked.

He thought before replying. 'Och yes,' he said. 'It would carry Nelson's Column, pigeons and all.'

In this fashion we recruited Alan Stuart and the Ford Anglia car. Which was the more reliable, Alan or the Anglia, I do not know. But I do know that I would go round the world with either of them, and there would be laughter and confidence all the way.

Forty years on.
Och. I'm speechless.

Chapter Seven

We were later in getting away than I had intended, for the arrival of Alan threw us off schedule. I was in a fever of impatience to be gone, which Kay's remote calm and Gavin's complacent confidence in no way soothed. At last, about seven in the evening, when we drove through Glasgow Cross and along London Road on the first mile of the road south, I was able to relax a little. Yet the relaxation was of a child going on a long anticipated holiday. Now and again it would come to me in the middle of a sentence, or in a moment of calm driving, that we really were going after the Stone, and I would hug the knowledge to me, a glowing secret whose warm presence I could feel. At the same time the knowledge steadied my excitment, for the cerebral part of the operation was past, and all that remained was to fulfil in action what had been created a thousand times in dreams. As I drove I knew that even the driving was all part of the unity of our operation.

I took the first spell in the Anglia with Alan at my side. Four hours before he had been a stranger, but now I had warmed to him and circumstances had made us old friends. I was glad of the opportunity to talk to him, and as I followed the rear light of Gavin's car down the long winding road to Carlisle, I told him how we intended to mate intention with success. He followed me carefully, and by the time we stopped at Gretna for a meal he knew exactly what his part would be when we came to the Abbey.

As we pushed through the blackness to Carlisle, the night became colder. It was plain to us that we were going to get hard frost with perhaps glazed ice on the higher stretches. Eight-horsepower cars are not the best vehicles for a four hundred mile journey in midwinter, but they turned back the miles constantly and uncomplainingly. Inside it was cold, and our breath froze on the windscreen, which had to be constantly wiped clear. Wrapped in our heavy coats we froze also. Yet time passed. We were all drivers,

46

and while two sat and slept or chatted or lit cigarettes for the drivers, the other two drove on steadily southwards.

We crossed the Border and looked back at the country we had left, and thought of our people snug in bed, for it was nearly midnight. I would have changed places with none of them, and as the draughts poked at us and our feet grew dead to heat and cold alike, we almost welcomed it as part of the great adventure. As the night wore on, the passengers became more silent, snatching half an hour's sleep before changing over to take another turn at the wheel. As we passed through Penrith and swung east for Scotch Corner, a fall of snow flurried across the headlights. We knew we were for it; the Pennines lay before us.

Before we were half way to the summit the snow came down in earnest. It was not honest snow, which lay crisply or drifted before the wind, but wet ice which congealed on everything it touched, like a black deadly skin. We slithered from corner to corner, driving by luck rather than judgement, until I gave up and passed the wheel to Alan, who was a much more competent driver than I. Again and again we were forced to stop to scrape the ice from the windcreen with our nails, for the wipers could not keep it clear. When we stopped on the summit to chip away the creeping ice on the cold glass, I had an idea.

'Remember that gill of rum we bought in Glasgow?' I asked. `Let's rub it on the glass, and the spirit will stop it from freezing up.' We did so, and drove on in a haze of alcohol.

As we ran down the other side of the Pennines conditions gradually improved. Soon we were running on soft ice which broke in slush and sang cheerfully under our wheels. But many times that night we knew the sickening sideways swing as the car slid across the road out of control. There were few other vehicles on the road, and it was one help all. Several times we helped to pull drivers out of the ditch, and more than once had the same assistance given to ourselves. The slow speed forced on us was all that saved the cars from damage.

We were well down in Nottinghamshire when dawn broke,

clear and frosty and welcome. We pulled in at a roadside cafe and had breakfast, at city prices, but welcome nevertheless, for we were starving. We washed as best we could in the frost, and the cold snapped at our skin. Although our eyes were heavy and our skin was grainy with sleeplessness, we joyfully filled our lungs and slapped our legs and stamped our feet, and proceeded on our way quite believing we were the four finest people in all that shining dawn.

It was afternoon when we reached London. We had been lost in its vast suburbs and lonely approaches. It was Kay's first visit to London, and I am sure she was not impressed. I think if it had been hers she would have swopped it all for five acres in Inverasdale, and while I would not wish to denigrate the eight million people who call it home, she would not have had a bad bargain.

We parked the cars behind the mammoth block of offices which the Government is building between Whitehall and the river. What we all needed was a wash and a meal, but we had no great time to lavish on luxuries. We went up to Lyons' Corner House and did the best we could in as short a time as possible, and then with considerable excitement we piled into the Anglia and shot along Whitehall, past Scotland Yard, so named as the place where Sir William Wallace was tortured to death, and from there to the Abbey.

We split into two parties, for we wanted to take no chances. Now that the attempt was to be made we felt that we could not be too careful. It would have crushed us if we had discovered that special security arrangements had been put into operation because of suspicions aroused by a group of four Scots who whispered and looked longingly at the Stone and measured every tomb and cranny east of Poets' Corner.

Gavin and I went first; Kay and Alan followed behind. It was a strange kirking. Kay had changed out of her slacks and looked very chic, but I felt that Alan's duffel coat looked a bit out of place in a church. He assured me that many well-dressed men wore them in England, and indeed my own observations confirmed this. Gavin's sports jacket and corduroys would have been more at home in a football crowd, but among the tourists he looked inconspicuous enough, if Gavin could ever look inconspicuous. He was the sort of person who made nuns cross themselves when they passed him in the street.

We approached the Abbey from the back and passed up the lane which runs from Old Palace Yard to Poets' Corner door. It was a quiet lane and quite suitable for our purpose, even although it was blocked by two iron gates. One of these gates was, I knew, never locked, and the other did not look as though it would last for long against my fine set of tools. Moreover, the door into the Abbey was not visible from the road. Here was our line of escape. We went into the Abbey and paced through the huge, dim, quiet extent of it. Its original austerity must have been breath-taking, but the severity of the line of the nave had been broken by frilly tombs and pompous statues. This was of considerable assistance to us, because apart from giving us cover, all the appendages, which cluttered up every available corner, would deaden any noise that we might make.

We paid the admission money to the chapels and followed the route I had already taken. Alan was worried by the six narrow wooden steps leading to the Confessor's Chapel, for, like me, he feared that we might not be able to manoeuvre the Stone down them. We both shrugged our shoulders at that. What had gone up must come down.

Now that we were there with intent, the Stone looked even larger than I had remembered. Would we really be able to lift such a massive thing? Just looking at its bulk made the whole thing seem impossible. Then an alternative method of getting it down from the five-foot high Confessor's Chapel suggested itself. Looking through the two glass doors of the rood-screen, we could see that the broad steps of the Sanctuary would present little difficulty to two, let alone three fairly able men. I had tried the doors on my previous visit, and I knew that they were not locked. The only snag to this plan was that the door we would have to use to get the Stone out of the Abbey was the Poets' Corner door, which would need to be forced, for it was padlocked in such a way that the lock could not be screwed off, even from inside. But that might not be too difficult. It was the only door to the Abbey made of pine. The rest were of oak, and as hard as whinstone.

We also paid considerable attention to the Coronation Chair, and to the barrier which prevented the public from pressing too closely against it. The latter would offer no trouble. It was hinged and would lift easily away, but the Chair would have to be damaged, for it fitted very closely round the Stone and the wooden flange along the front seemed thicker and stouter on further examination. I decided to try partially to dismantle it with a screwdriver during the night, lest the necessity for speed should force us to tear it apart with a jemmy. The English have run the risk of having their Chair damaged ever since they built it to receive stolen property, but nonetheless we wanted to keep damage to a minimum.

Leaving the Chapel, we passed the plain, unadorned tomb of Edward I of England, who had ravaged our country and removed the Stone six hundred and fifty years before. 'Keep Troth' was his motto. It was a command to others; never a rule of his own conduct. He was as treacherous a Plantagenet as ever raped a child or lied in his teeth. He had coveted our country, and two countries which should have lived in peace had fought a series of bloody wars, the memory of which could never quite be effaced from the minds of the two peoples. Six hundred years is a long time, but there was a continuity of strife from his time to ours, and his sacking of the Abbey of Scone was, I hoped, to have its more civilised counterpart here in Westminster that very night.

When we got outside, we found that a grey haar had crept in with the darkness, and the night bore that cold cheerlessness which raw frost brings to a big city. The shops, however, were gay with lights, and each pub and each cafe had tricked itself out in tinsel and coloured paper. Christmas was all about us, scarcely the Christmas of the clean snow, the stall and the little Child, but a

Christmas nevertheless. Suddenly I felt that perhaps we were all part of a new Christmas Carol, and that the little man with the pinched face who stood wistfully looking at the great Christmas tree in Trafalgar Square was really Bob Cratchit on his way home to his children in Camden Town. The moment passed, and again we found ourselves there as strangers, lost to the wonder they all shared. We went among these revellers to Lyons Corner House in the Strand, and sat there with them. There, among their celebrations, we held a council of war.

Our first point of discussion was whether or not we should take action that night or wait until the following day, which was Sunday and Christmas Eve. I pointed out that we had had no sleep that night, and, if things went according to plan, we should have no sleep for at least two nights after the operation. I reminded them also that, although there was every sign of revelry around us, the pubs would be open even later on Sunday in celebration of Christmas Eve, and the police would be more occupied with drunks then than they were tonight. The English are no respecters of the Sabbath.

Kay, however, had one eye on the purse, and was not keen to stay in London a moment longer than was necessary. Gavin wanted to 'have a bash' and Alan was no less keen. I agreed. Although I was tired, I was also excited. I was aching to start, and at times tiredness is no bad thing. I am a nervous person, and nervous people are less frightened if they are tired. The reactions are a trifle slower. There is an extra fraction of time between impact and reaction which allows a calculated response and can prevent that swift instinctive movement, which is not always wise and is occasionally cowardly. There is never a better time than now.

We paid our bill and left. I had a long eerie vigil in front of me, but my stomach was full and my mind was clear. Alan and Kay drove off in the Anglia to make themselves familiar with the route west out of London, for it was their duty to head for Dartmoor with the Stone early the following morning. We said au revoir with a carelessness that was quite unassumed, and it was not until they were gone that I realised that if things went wrong I would not see them again until I had passed through prison.

The starlings were raising their ceaseless shrill chattering in the eaves of the buildings as Gavin and I turned into Northumberland Avenue where our old Ford was parked. I raked in my grip and produced the tools of my new profession: a file, a saw, a screw-driver bit, a wrench, a hooded torch, a length of wire, a tin of vaseline to lubricate the saw, and, of course, the jemmy. I had gathered them together as symbols of my resolution. I had handled them a hundred times. I had fawned on them and looked at them and loved them far more than I had ever loved any inanimate thing. Their value as symbols was past. They had now become real.

Gavin sat watching me as I stowed them about me. The car was small, and as I stretched and stowed I felt that the eyes of all the passers-by were upon me. I had to go outside to put the jemmy in position, for it was too long to manoeuvre easily. Once I had it in the sling I had to be careful how I moved, for it galled me sorely in the groin. When I had my coat on all was hidden except a slight stoutness which Gavin made jokes about as we drove along the Embankment.

My laughter was strained and I would have preferred silence. I have an antipathy to working in company, and this time I would especially have preferred solitude because I was nervous and frightened. Yet the fear turned into excitement as we neared the Abbey and I had to screw it down until it was only a pressure along my ribs, occasionally unwinding itself in an involuntary twitch. I do not know if Gavin knew I was nervous. Perhaps he did and was trying to jolly me along. But I tried to hide it from him for his sympathy would have been unbearable.

We parked the car in the Sanctuary, the open space outside the west door. With a brief 'Cheerio' to Gavin I eased myself out of the car, galling my groin on the jemmy as I did so. Then I stood for a moment and adjusted my dress before leaving and walking casually towards the west door. Big Ben struck 5.15 p.m. We were on time.

I passed out of the shining noisy darkness of a London evening.

Inside, the light was soft yet it seemed to illuminate me and probe me out as a persistent and sinister visitor. I pulled my heavy coat about me and hated the damning jemmy at my side.

Followed at a distance by Gavin I walked slowly up the north transept, pausing only to gaze at a Latin inscription, or read an English one. The venerable guide was in conversation with a woman and he paid no attention to me. I walked on into the shadows, which seemed to be patches of only slightly less intense light.

I turned as I reached the top of the north transept. It was in comparative darkness. A low rail separated me from the extreme end of the transept, where, under the brief cover of a cleaner's trolley, I hoped to hide. Down in the aisle, Gavin walked slowly past. No one else was in sight. He nodded to me briefly, absentmindedly. I crawled under the trolley and having covered my face with my coat lay perfectly still.

Forty years on

We travel great distances, winter and summer, nowadays cursing the roads and the traffic. In those days travel was still something of an adventure. Snow and ice were regarded as natural hazards about which nothing could be done. Cars were draughty boxes on wheels. We had not learned the trick of carrying nightlights, small stubby candles, a row of which burning under the windscreen kept it unfrozen. A few years later cars started to have heaters, but it was into the sixties before gritting of roads became commonplace. Even then it was done by a man standing on the back of a lorry, and swinging the stuff off with a shovel.

What was not commonplace was the purpose of our travel. I hope that old age, if I should ever reach that state, will never wither me into agreeing with the absurd proposition that youth is wasted on the young. Ours certainly wasn't. Such an aphorism is fit only for those who as youngsters wasted their youth by playing the saner part, and to quote Chesterton, 'kept their head and kept their heart and only lost their soul.' Youth, like any of the ages of life, is for living, and the four of us were doing just that.

53

Chapter Eight

My own little world was under my coat collar, where the steam from my breath condensed on my face and the saliva from the corner of my mouth crept along my sleeve. The hard stone of the Abbey floor was part of it, but the greatest reality was my heart, which thudded and pounded and threatened to stick in my throat and make me vomit.

This, I had always reckoned, would be the most dangerous and trying part. To be caught at any time would be bad enough, but to be caught with my pockets stuffed with house-breaking tools before I had had a chance even to touch the Stone would be ignominy and derision. And I was young enough to fear derision more than anything else.

Gradually I relaxed. My leg ceased to twitch and although I wanted to cough I forced the need into an attic of my mind. Quarter to six struck, and then the hour. Gavin would now be out of the building for it closed at six. My head was still covered and I could not see whether or not the lights were out. I did not dare to look.

When quarter past six struck I tensed and looked up. The lights were out and I was in darkness. I could now move in safety to St Paul's Chapel, where, since it was under repair, I was certain I could hide without fear of discovery.

I listened, and, hearing nothing but the vague susurration of the traffic in the world outside, crept stiffly from my hiding-place. I took off my shoes for silence, and my stockinged feet were noiseless on the cold stone floor. A hundred and fifty feet above me the great vaulted roof soared in the darkness, invisible like a clouded sky. You could reach out and touch the silence as I started to creep along.

I had gone three paces when I suddenly heard a noise. It was the jangling of keys, and even as I listened, a light swept round a corner of the transept and came towards me. Shocked and frightened, I crouched behind a statue, hoping the watchman would miss me.

The jangling stopped and the light shone in my face. I looked up, white and piteous.

'What the devil are you doing here?' The watchman's voice was clear and masterful, like the voice of a public speaker. He was tall and bearded, and suddenly I knew that he had been badly frightened. He was restoring his self confidence by being over-bearing in the presence of the poor moron that he saw before him.

'I've been shut in,' I said, hanging my head on my chest, and making myself smaller and more like a mouse than usual.

'Why didn't you shout then?' he asked. He was not bullying me, and although he sounded as though he spoke with all the authority of the House of Lords, his voice was not unkind.

'I thought I'd get a row,' I said, and my voice quivered on the verge of tears. He told me that this would never do, and I cringed before him. Then he saw my shoes in my hand, and I had to tell him the truth, as I could think of no lie.

'I was frightened someone would hear me, 'I said, 'And come and catch me.'

'Well, put them on,' he said. 'You're lucky I didn't hit you over the head. I'm patrolling about here all night, you know.'

For the first time a wild hope flamed up in me that perhaps he would put me out without handing me over to the police, who would be bound to search me. Then as I stooped to put on my shoes, the jemmy slipped from the sling under my armpit, and only my arm pressing against my side, kept it from falling with a clang onto the stone paving of the Abbey floor.

I held it there in a sort of left-sided palsy, and then suddenly we were moving towards the door, the west door, through which I had entered with excitement and pride only an hour before. As we reached the door, he suddenly shot a question at me.

'What's your name?'

'John Alison,' I replied, with a bland ability to improvise which amazed me.

'Your address?'

'Care of Fee, 49 Arlington Street, N 14.'

He noted it down on the back of his Post Office Savings Bank book. Then a thought seemed to strike him.

'Have you any money?'

I told him I had a pound.

'You're sure,' he insisted. 'You weren't sheltering in the Abbey because you had nowhere else to go?'

'No,' I said. I did not feel that I looked like a down-and-out.

Then he opened the door, led me down the steps, and with a kindly word and a 'Merry Christmas`, he let me out into the concourse of people who had nothing on their conscience. I hitched the jemmy back into its sling but I did not dare to lift my head and step out like a free man until I was far from the Abbey.

My first reaction was one of jubilation that I had won free of a dicey event. I had showed my willingness to take risks if not my ability to succeed. I had met the most unfavourable of situations, and coped with it with an ability to lie which rather shocked me, but gave me not a little pride as well.

When, from the far side of Parliament Square, I turned and had a last look at the massive building which had almost been my prison, I realised that the Stone was still inside, and I wondered at my temerity and sneered at my complacency. With amazing folly I had thought that I might do something of note and of wonder, and I had only made myself ridiculous. I envied people who had someone to tell them what to do next, and walked on defeated.

Then I thought of the night-watchman with whom I had crossed swords and scored a contemptible victory. The honours had all been on my side, but so had the advantages, for I knew all that went on, and was fighting for a cause and striving for my own personal liberty, while he was only patrolling for pay. He had treated me gently and courteously; he had set me free when he could have exerted his petty authority. Yet when it came out in what circumstances we had met, he would become the reproach of his superiors, and the gibe of his equals. Added to my misery was the thought that if a real victory lay between us as two humans that night, the victory was his. He had acted at Christmas time in a true Christmas spirit; he had made no room for me in his church, but he had seen that I was not penniless when he turned me away. The fact that I had to accept his kindness as a sort of betrayal of him troubled me greatly, and I could find little consolation in knowing that the whole sorry business arose from this un-Christian English church keeping property at Westminster which did not belong to it. I greatly admire gentleness as a virtue, and I met gentleness in the Abbey that evening.

I walked aimlessly along the Embankment, resigned to a long wait, for we had made no provision to meet should things go wrong. It had never occurred to me that I might be caught and ejected, and that a rendezvous point would be necessary, and, somehow, I had to stop the others trying to make contact with me inside the Abbey when zero hour approached. I was much criticised by many of my friends for my lack of foresight in this instance, but foresight can only see through a fog. Hindsight is the only clear vision. We had not been planning for failure. We had been planning for success. However by one of the series of coincidences which were to mark everything we did, I found Gavin's car, which I had left only two hours before. It was standing on the Embankment, and I waited beside it in the bitter frost and drew on a cigarette. I knew that Gavin would arrive shortly and I would have to explain how I had bungled matters and let everyone down.

After about quarter of an hour I saw him coming jauntily towards me. He wore no coat, but his hands were lost in a massive pair of sheep-skin gloves. A cigarette poked skywards from the corner of his mouth. He was almost on me before he saw me, and then he stopped dead in his tracks and the cigarette fell to the pavement.

'How did you get here?' he asked as he stooped to pick it up. His amazement was justified. He knew I had been locked in the Abbey.

'I walked,' I said sourly and ungraciously.

He unlocked the car door and we both got in.

'I got caught,' I said, and told him the story. He listened to me to the end without a word, and then he started the car and drove off.

'You can thank your lucky stars you're not in there.' He jerked a fur-clad thumb towards the bulk of New Scotland Yard, which loomed over us. I was too dejected to reply.

We parked the car in Northumberland Avenue and moved over to Trafalgar Square, where Gavin had arranged to meet Kay and Alan after their return from making themselves familiar with the west road out of London.

We waited moodily at the Underground entrance in the Square. They were late, and I was in no mood for conversation. As the minutes dragged by it seemed to me that there had been another hitch, and that Alan and Kay would never materialise out of the thousands who teemed about the giant Christmas tree in the breeze-blown spray of Trafalgar's fountains. I moved away from Gavin and watched the crowds and listened to the great noise which was soothing in its strength and impersonality. When I came back to the subway feeling less of a failure, I found Gavin talking to Kay and Alan. He was explaining what had happened.

Nothing more was said about the Stone for we were all feeling pretty sick. Alan, with a cheerfulness which was not faked, and which did not grate, suggested that we should cross over the road and 'eat our Christmas dinners.' It was only a few hours since we had fed, but we all suddenly realised that it was good advice. The human body seems to be able to go without sleep for lengthy periods, but the longer the period the more food is required. In the last stages of the expedition, when I had only cat-napped during a period of over a hundred hours, I found myself eating ravenously and continuously. After the meal, we crossed over Northumberland Avenue and sat in the Anglia and held a council of war.

I told them in detail what had happened. Among the remarks the watchman had made to me was one which filled us all with dismay. He had told me that it was a dangerous business being in the Abbey after hours, for there were watchmen prowling round all night.

To me this did not ring true. My information was that there was only one watchman, and I could not see him doing his rounds more than once every two hours. But on the face of it it was plausible. After all, I had been caught. My information might have been false, and if the watchman were correct we might as well press the starter and go home.

We considered trying the same plan again the following night, but gave it up as too dangerous. I could have wept with impotence and shame. Here we sat in the centre of London; reivers, moss-troopers, pseudo men of action, frustrated by one bearded watchman. It seemed to me that we had failed, but it was unthinkable that we should go home yet. On the other hand a coarse and blundering attempt could only end in further failure, and bring disrepute down on our country and on ourselves.

'Don't forget we are wasting money,' I said. 'And the man who gave us it can ill afford it.'

Kay's voice came from the back of the car. 'There are still more nights and more chances.'

'We might break in from the outside,' said Alan, who had not shown the slightest dismay at our initial failure.

'Or we might try a cheeky attempt in daylight,' I added, forgetting my cautious thoughts of a moment before.

Alan summed up what we all thought.

'Bruce watched his spider seven times. We've only tried once. Let's go along to the Abbey and look for spiders.'

We all laughed. Gavin started the engine and we turned into Whitehall and made once again for the Abbey.

We stopped the car in Old Pie Street, and Gavin and Alan got out. I stayed with Kay for I did not want to be seen twice on the same night by the same watchman. The other two went off to prowl around and glean what information they could. They penetrated to the Dean's Yard, and from the Dean's Yard to the

Cloisters, and returned to report that they had seen nothing but a drunken Cockney lying in the gateway from the Sanctuary to the Dean's Court.

'We didn't think it was the Dean himself,' said Alan. 'So we passed by on the other side.'

We made several other excursions that night, but they were all as fruitless as the first, and towards eleven o'clock we decided to call it a day. We knew that in Glasgow our friends would be waiting and wondering and anxious, and wanting some report from us, but we had little to report to them, and we saw no reason to telephone them to tell them that we had failed. We went instead for some hot coffee, because the temperature was dropping fast, and indeed London was in for one of its coldest nights for many years.

It was now late and the streets were full of drunks. The whole West End was jammed with people determined on having a good time to celebrate the birth of Christ, no matter how much it cost them. We eased the car through them and swore at them, for there were many who were clumsy in drink. Time and again we pondered on their reactions should they know why we were among them. We felt like a bubble of Scotland in the centre of a hostile stream.

It was now imperative that we should find somewhere to sleep, for it was getting late and we were very tired. Kay was adamant on the subject.

'We can't go back to Glasgow with all our money spent and no Stone. We'll sleep in the cars and save three pounds.'

The temperature was ten degrees below outside, and our breath was freezing on the windows. We had had only snatches of sleep for thirty-six hours and none of us had been warm since we left Glasgow. Murder might have been in our hearts as we turned on Kay, but underlying her economy was a strange truth. In the cars we lived as a sort of community of mutual support. Together in the cars we preserved our fragment of Scotland and our comradeship and our integrity of purpose, all of which we might have lost had we sought warmth and soft beds.

We drove to a side turning past the Albert Hall, and pulled into the parking space in the centre of the road, one car nose to tail behind the other. It must have been well into the early hours of Christmas Eve by now, for the streets were much quieter. In the hotel opposite to where we sat, the manager came hopefully to the door at the sound of car engines, and seeing two shabby little cars, encrusted with mud, prepared to refuse us a bed. To his obvious anger, however, we did not get out of the cars, and after a while he went to an upstairs window, whence he glared balefully down at us. Plenty of people spent the night in their cars when touring, so there was nothing he could do to harm us.

With our breath freezing on anything we breathed on, we settled down to pass the night.

Forty years on

It cannot escape anyone's notice with what kindness the Abbey watchman treated me. I never met him again. I like to think that he was a trainee curate, and that he settled into a quiet country living, and became beloved of his flock, and never read the works of Tom Paine or Samuel Butler, and was never troubled by philosophic doubts. He represents the Church of England I admire. I have a tiny copy of the Book of Common Prayer, *the Cranmer and Latimer one, which I read from time to time. I love it. A smile of affection comes to my lips when I think of the Church of England and its night-watchman. A Presbyterian beadle would have kicked my arse all the way to the church door.*

The watchman's concern that I might have no money strikes a chord dissonant with the days we now live in. Abbeys remain shut while many of the youth of the country sleep rough in London streets. London is richer now than it has ever been. Unless they are very careful, a people who grow rich grow away from the common humanity of us all. I hope that that never happens in Scotland.

Chapter Nine

I have never been so cold in my life. If this was martyrdom, I preferred the fire of the stake. London was in one of its periodic Moscow moods, and I swear I saw wolves scavenging the streets. Feet, ears and hands we had long since ceased to worry about, but now it seemed impossible to keep up body heat. We were not dressed for palavering about in Arctic conditions, and with no engine to give its meagre heat our breath froze immediately on the windows. In the car in front Kay and Alan had the luxury of a travelling rug, but in our car, Gavin and I had to make do with an old coat. The night developed into a struggle for that coat.

Every half hour throughout the night one or other of us, in either of the cars, would waken up and start the engine and race through the streets, hoping to find a coffee stall or an early morning cafe. Gavin and I had to be particularly careful, as our car had no anti- freeze, and a burst cylinder would have ruined the expedition. We were all heartily glad when six o'clock came, and we decided to go somewhere, try to eat breakfast, and thaw out.

At breakfast we were not so much cold, as stiff and twisted and petrified into distorted shapes. We must have looked like four Highland reivers as we sat, miserable and silent, eating our congealed sausages. We all still wore our coats. Gavin and I wore heavy overcoats and a growth of stubble on our chins. Alan was hidden in the depths of a duffel coat, from which every now and again he peered like a wren out of a nest, to invite us to 'spend your holidays in the sunny south.' Kay managed her mug while dressed in scarf, polo neck, slacks and gloves, and the waiter was not impressed. However, we kept talking about our long cold run up from Ilfracombe, and no doubt he took pity on us.

We lingered over breakfast to the last possible moment, and then drove aimlessly round the city, for it was very early on Sunday morning, and no one was abroad. We did not know that by this time tomorrow we would have made off with the Stone, but each of us knew in our hearts that we were going to have another try. When the streets began to stir, we parked the cars in Northumberland Avenue, and went up to Charing Cross station to look for baths. Take a cold, demoralised man and give him a jug of hot water and a razor, and if he is worth his salt, he will be spring heeled and glowing inside ten minutes; give him a bath and he will be a superman.

There are no baths at Charing Cross so we took a tube across to Waterloo. It was magnificent. We lay and steeped until the attendant came and thumped on the doors and abused us. British Rail seem to pick their minor officials for their rudeness, but it was just as well. Not having relaxed for forty eight hours or more, it would have been fatal had we steeped until we were soft and sleepy.

Sleep was indeed far from us. When we were clean and warm we held a council of war. We were all uneasy, for we were spending a lot of money. We would have felt inadequate for the rest of our lives had we been forced to creep back ignominiously over the Border, having had a cheap holiday at a friend's expense. On the other hand we did not wish to force ourselves into rash and clumsy action. Alan and Gavin wanted very sensibly to leave the next attempt until night-time, when, with all the knowledge we had gleaned, we might force an entry from the outside. I thought, however, that this was scarcely possible, and I wanted at least to consider a daylight attempt. The twenty year old plan evolved, I think, by Compton MacKenzie and Councillor Gray in the days of their youth, had been to create a diversion in the nave while a party of men attacked the Stone and carried it out the back door of the Margaret Chapel.

We had rejected a daylight attempt before as being impracticable, but in the absence of any other we decided to investigate it. We spent the day in and around the Abbey, which was filled with Christmas worshippers, for it was Christmas Eve. At one point we even posted Kay just off Knightsbridge in the Anglia, in case we got a chance to seize the Stone and arrived to transfer it to her with the police hard on our rear number plate. None of us, however, seriously considered it a possibility, except Kay, perhaps, who sat waiting with that imperturbable calmness which was such a feature of her character. However, when we arrived back at Kay some three hours later, we had no Stone, and again it seemed that we were beaten. And time was wearing on. It was late in the afternoon of the day before Christmas.

But now, more than ever, our failure became a challenge to win through. We had been many hours in London, and our only anchor to Scotland was the Stone, so surely set in the heart of the Abbey. It had taken on its own character, and it seemed to us to be something venerable in the hands of its enemies, and as we mingled with the sightseers and read the inscriptions to half forgotten Englishmen and knew in our hearts that a daylight attack was impossible, we were ever on the look-out for that scrap of information which would give us a clue to a raid in the hours of darkness.

Dusk fell on a raw frozen night, with no cheer in the bright lights which lost themselves in a faint freezing mist. Before the next dawn we were to succeed, but we did not know it then. We were pretty miserable. Laugh, you bastards, laugh, at the idea of four youngsters raiding the heart of the Empire, with no money, no back-up team and no headquarters other than an old car, but we persisted. Sitting in the car in Northumberland Avenue we held another of our interminable councils of war, searching for the loophole we felt there must be in the Abbey guard.

At the end of the council we went for a meal, and in the restaurant Kay drew me aside. She was white-faced and shivering, and I suddenly noticed she was far from well.

'What's the trouble, Kay?' I asked. I knew she was hardy, and I was troubled to see her looking so ill.

'Of all the things,' she said almost casually, 'I've got the flu. I've been feeling ill all day, and I'm running a temperature now.'

I was horrified. I am never ill, and therefore fear illness, and this one, coming on the eve of our next attempt, seemed inevitably to mean the end of the expedition. The very private thought crossed my mind that it gave us the perfect excuse. While our first loyalty was to carry through to the end, I did not see how we could stay in London while Kay suffered. What more could be expected of us?

While all these thoughts shot through my head I was standing staring at Kay. Before I had time to frame any words she continued,

'Do you think that if we don't decide to do anything tonight, I could sleep in a hotel?'

I suggested that she might be better to go home, but she would not hear of it. I think she felt that she was now the weak link in our chain, and she was determined that no matter how overstrained she was she would not break and let us down. I did not express my admiration for her, and she would have been embarrassed had I attempted to do so.

'Don't,' she pleaded as we walked to our table, 'tell Gavin and Alan. There's no use upsetting them.'

After dinner, I told the other two that I was determined that Kay should have at least a few hours sleep in a hotel that night, and they heartily agreed. We decided to relax for a little while first, and we went for a drink to a pub up near Victoria. I think we were all racking our brains and turning over in our heads all the knowledge we had, to try to see what to do next, while all around us people were celebrating peace on earth and good will towards men. I can think of many reasons to get drunk, but the birth of Christ is not one of them. None at all is a better one than that. However, gradually the warmth and companionship around us affected us, and for a little time we forgot all about failure and enjoyed ourselves.

Towards nine o'clock I drove Kay over to St. Pancras and found a hotel for her. It was a miserable little doss-house, but it was cheap and she would hear of none better. Indeed, we had not the money for anything better. She was controlling her illness remarkably well, and I don't think either of the other boys ever discovered how she was feeling. Before I left her, she extracted from me the most solemn and binding promise that if there was to be any excitement whatsoever I would telephone her. I carefully noted the telephone number and gave her the promise, never thinking just how much excitement that promise was to yield.

I went back to Gavin and Alan, and we made our usual journey along Whitehall to the Abbey. It was now certain that if we were to be successful we would have to break in from the outside. Yet again we marshalled the facts that we knew. Firstly, the door to Poets' Corner, the most secluded door to the Abbey, was of pine and could possibly be forced. Secondly, there was at least one watchman inside. Thirdly, if the information given to me when I was caught on Saturday were correct, he kept up a patrol all night, and could reasonably be expected to hear the noise we made forcing the door, and would come across us in any event, even if he did not hear our first forced entry.

These were the relevant considerations. The rest was a matter of deduction. None of us could really believe that a watchman, unsupervised as he would certainly be, would pad continuously about the dim corridors of the Abbey. He would need to be a religious fanatic to do that, and he had seemed a nice human sort of person to me. The most he could be expected to do was patrol at regular intervals, and whether or not he did so would be a matter for his own diligence. For my part, I could not see him doing his rounds any oftener than every two hours. At what time these patrols would take place we did not know, and that was our problem.

We needed more definite information. It was now after ten o'clock, and Alan and Gavin slipped out of the car and walked boldly into the Dean's Yard to see what they could discover. From the Dean's Yard, they pushed on into the Cloisters, looking and talking like two interested, if belated, tourists. In a fret of over caution I had warned them that anyone who saw them would take their names, as my name had already been taken, but as very often happens the bold plan succeeded.

They had been in the Cloisters only a few minutes when they

were approached by an elderly divine, who later volunteered that he was Archdeacon Marriot.

"Rather late to be in here,' observed the old gentleman peering at them nervously.

'It is indeed,' Alan agreed. 'But we are very interested in the building. We're wondering if it's dry rot that makes the surface of the stone peel off like that,' and he pointed to where the centuries had eaten into the stonework.

The Archdeacon looked. 'Age,' he said. 'It's age.'

The Archdeacon, a real enthusiast for his church, seized Alan by the arm, and took him round to show him some more of the interesting features of the Cloisters, and Alan, a civil engineer, plied him with leading questions.

The discourse had scarcely begun when the night watchman, the same bearded fellow whom I had already met, appeared out of what was obviously his office in the north-west corner of the Cloisters.

The Archdeacon halted his discourse to speak to the watchman.

'I thought you went off at ten o'clock,' he said.

'Eleven o'clock, sir,' replied the watchman respectfully.

'Oh yes,' said the Archdeacon. 'Then Dandy or Hyslop comes on.' He turned from the watchman and resumed his discourse on Norman arches, flying buttresses, and the Perpendicular style.

The two boys heard him to a finish, anxious to get away with this information about the watchman. It was of the first magnitude, and they knew its value. When he had finished his discourse, the Archdeacon beamed amiably on them and asked what part of Scotland they had come from.

'Eh! Eh! Forgandenny,' said Alan seizing on the place where he had been to school, and which he thought was the least likely the Archdeacon would know.

'Forgandenny,' boomed the divine. 'I know it very well.' Alan's heart sank to his boots as the Archdeacon continued: 'I once had a living near there. Do you know So-and-so and So-and-so?'

Hastily Gavin explained that it was a long time since they had been at home. Seizing the gentleman's hand, he shook it, and the two boys departed into the night, feeling a little guilty at having deceived such a venerable and charming old man.

Again we sat in the car, our cigarettes glowing in the darkness. We now had enough information to press on. We knew with certainty that there was only one night watchman, who was relieved at eleven o'clock. We could be almost certain that he would not patrol oftener than every two hours, and we were willing to gamble on that. Furthermore, the new watchman would probably spend some time talking to the retiring one, and we estimated that his rounds would take place about 11.45, 1.45. and 3.45. In actual fact we overestimated his efficiency. The only patrols he made were at 11.45 p.m. and 6.15 a.m.

There was also another factor. All around us were signs of the wildest conviviality, amounting to drunkenness. We did not know the incidence of sobriety among nightwatchmen, but we did not think it would be high. There was always the chance that the new watchman had blunted his perceptions by spending his evening in a pub. If so, it would make our job easier. We waited patiently outside the Dean's Yard, hoping to see the incoming watchman pass reeling and hiccupping, but we saw no one like that. At any rate, we now knew that if we could choose a time when he was in his office, he would not hear us at Poets' Corner door, or anywhere else near the Stone. We had identified that his office in the Cloisters was too far away.

It was now nearly midnight, and we should really have collected Kay, but there was still a great amount of spadework to be done, and we felt that she deserved a sleep. I was loth to disturb her, sick as she was, until we actually needed her. We decided to do our initial preparation without her.

The lane leading to the door we intended to force was defended by two gates. The one which opened directly onto Old Palace Yard stood wide open, but the other, ten yards from the Abbey door, was locked and bolted. Moreover, a gas lamp threw its light directly on to this gate and on to the door. A twist in the lane, a line of railings and a flying buttress gave reasonable cover to the door, but the gate was in full view of the road. At the top of the lane, and on the outside of the gate, there was a little space where a small car could be manoeuvred, and sitting with its lights off, it might pass unnoticed from the road. But there was still the gate to be circumvented or forced open. Lifting the Stone over it was out of the question.

We now turned to examine that side of the lane which was closest to the Abbey, and indeed to the Margaret Chapel, which I knew well from the inside. A wooden hoarding, breached by a padlocked door, fenced off a little space hard against the Abbey wall. This space was in use by masons as a yard for their repairs to the fabric of the building. We reckoned that if we forced the door in this hoarding, and passed through the sheds, it would bring us out past the lamplit gate, and directly opposite Poets' Corner door.

It was too early to attempt this, as the streets were still full. The pubs had just skailed, and we were delighted to see that insobriety was the rule of the night rather than the exception. That would keep the police busy. We left the cars and walked about, calling out a hearty 'Merry Christmas' to everyone we passed.

As time melted away, we became more and more tense and strung up. Conditions were ideal, for there was an air of careless well-being in the city. The Cabinet Minister took out his cigar, and the policeman unbuttoned his tunic. This was London, the heart of the Empire. London was preparing to celebrate another Christmas. The Union Jacks were flying: all was right with the world.

Forty years on
I confess that as I type this up, I am dying to know what happened next.

Chapter Ten

When two o'clock struck, we knew that the time had come. A few people still sang through the streets, but they were a camouflage rather than a danger. They were a warm kindly people, and they often shouted greetings to us, as country people do, and I warmed to them and felt that had conditions been different we could have initiated them into the rites of the ceilidh and had a night with them. The faults of Scotland, dear Jimmy, lie not with the English, but with ourselves, for we have made ourselves underlings.

But conditions were not different, and our warm amiability towards them was only a patina on our inward selves. Excitement had gone, and with it our sickness and fear. I suppose our defence mechanisms were deadened by fatigue, for while we calculated risks, we could weigh them only in relation to the end, and not as risks to ourselves or to our liberty. It was as well that it were so, for had we stopped to think of Wormwood Scrubs or Dartmoor, our purpose might have been blunted.

As the last chimes of Big Ben died away, I produced my jemmy, and Gavin and Alan went up the lane with it towards the door in the wooden hoarding. I stood at the bottom, feigning drunkenness, and broke into a fit of coughing whenever I saw anyone coming. When I coughed, they flattened into the shadows close to the hoarding.

I heard a creak which ended silently, and then a whispered shout. The square was deserted, and I crept up the lane to join them. The hasp and padlock hung at an angle from the door. We wrenched them off and passed in.

We found ourselves in a typical mason's yard, with all the tools of the trade scattered round. Straight ahead was a little stone stair leading up to the back door to the Margaret Chapel.

I crept up the stair, keeping well below the stone balustrade, for before I had mounted three steps I was out of cover of the hoarding, and in full view of the road. The door was of solid oak, studded with iron. I tried the jemmy on it. A toothpick would have been as effective. Regretfully I crawled back down.

To our left, as we faced the Abbey, and extending towards Poets' Corner, was a line of low sheds, and we next investigated these. In the dim glow of my hooded torch we crept through the eerie darkness. On both sides were work benches, loaded with stone and drawings, and we were careful to make no noise, for at any moment we expected to see a burly watchman leaping from the shadows.

We were brought up short by a door, but a door in a lean-to shed was nothing to our magnificent jemmy. We opened it leaving scarcely a mark and making no sound at all. We stepped out into shadow, rounded a corner, and stopped short of a dazzling patch of light. There, brown and solid before us, was the door to Poets' Corner. We had successfully outflanked the bolted gate.

We went no further, for it was not yet time to assail the door. We had to get Kay from her hotel, and we had to wait until such time as we felt certain that the watchman had just completed his rounds. But the important thing to us was not just that we had found our way to a door which we knew could not stop us; it was that we had set in motion the first of a series of events which were to force us to go on and on and on, until we either succeeded, or, as seemed very likely then, were caught. We had started trying at last.

We retreated the way we had come and closed the doors behind us. We stuck the hasp on the outside gate close to the wood, so that only a thorough examination would show that it had been tampered with. Then we walked boldly down the lane, swaying a little, and crooning softly, like three drunks who had just completed private business against the wooden hoarding.

Our next task was to arouse Kay. It was not a pleasant one, for no hotel keeper likes to be aroused at three o'clock in the morning. It annoys them. We drove round to the telephone boxes outside the Central Hall, but although I let the number ring for more than five minutes there was no reply. We jumped back into the cars. I drove the old Ford with Alan by my side, and Gavin drove the Anglia, a disposition which was to affect our later plans. As we drove to St. Pancras we talked blithely of using the jemmy on the door of the hotel, if they would not let Kay out.

Alan and I pulled up outside the hotel, while Gavin waited round the corner. I got out and hammered on the door. At length a basement window opened. 'What do you want?' said a voice.

'I want Miss Warren,' I said. Sir Victor Warren, the Lord Provost of Glasgow, was tied completely to London control of Scotland. Kay had felt that a Lord Provost should win some distinction in his life, so she had registered under the name of Victoria Warren. I expect that that is all he will be remembered for.

There was a spate of grumbles, and I apologised profusely.

'I've just had word that my father's ill,' I said, feeling that it was a poor lie, 'and we've got to leave for Scotland right away.'

'All right. All right,' complained the voice. 'I'll go and tell her.'

I went out and sat in the car beside Alan. The end of the jemmy was in my trouser pocket, with its haft buttoned up under my jacket. It gave me a comfortable feeling to know that very shortly we would be using it on the door of Westminster Abbey.

A man came along the road, climbed the steps to the hotel and knocked on the door. The light splashed out across the pavement. He passed in and his shadow crossed the threshold behind him. The door closed.

'Well! Well!' said Alan, slightly scandalised. 'That man got in easily enough.'

I thought of my knuckles bruised from beating on the door.

'My knock can't have had the right accent,' I said ruefully.

'He's probably reaping where you put in all the spade work,' said Alan, getting his metaphors mixed.

As we waited for Kay, we discussed what business could bring yet another caller to the hotel at this hour of the morning. Truly, we thought, this was not at all the type of hotel for a lady to stay in.

Meanwhile, in the hotel, Kay had left her door slightly ajar. Suddenly she heard downstairs the soft single ring as a telephone receiver was lifted. The voice of the hotel manager was so faint that she could make out only a word or two, but it was enough to convince her that he was telephoning the police.

She dressed hurriedly, not knowing what was amiss, but fearful that something had happened to put us in danger. Before she was able to warn us, the front door opened and the man we had already seen passed in.

She listened intently, and was able to piece together what was going on. The landlord, suspicious of us and of the telephone call at 3 a.m., had telephoned the police, since he believed that we had put Kay into the hotel while we went to commit some crime. He was not an unobservant man.

Outside, we continued to laugh and joke rather uneasily. Then the door opened and the stranger came straight down the steps towards us. He flashed a Metropolitan Police Warrant Card under my nose.

I'm a detective,' he said.

My stomach convulsed and my palms sweated. There is nothing like a guilty conscience for giving you a feeling of guilt.

'Do you mind if I take some details?' he continued, going to the top of his list of rhetorical questions.

'Of course,' I said, meaning the opposite. 'Is there anything wrong?'

'Only routine,' he replied. 'Can I see your driving licence'

I fished it out and gave it to him. He took down my name and address.

'What's the trouble?' I asked, rather testily. The jemmy in my pocket seemed as big as a tree trunk.

'You realise,' he said, 'that this is Christmas Eve, and thousands of people are in the West End with no transport to take them home?'

'I dare say,' I said. 'But I'm not lending them my car.'

'As it is, several hundred cars have already been stolen.' He looked at me. I stared back coldly.

'What is the number of your car?'

He emphasised the words 'is' and 'your' just sufficiently to let me see that he thought I had stolen the car.

Like a fool I had forgotten to memorise the number. 'I don't know,' I said. 'I hired it.'

His questions got more and more difficult, for I could give him neither the name nor the address of the garage it came from. That had been Gavin's part of the preparations, and although he sat just round the corner I did not want to refer the detective to him, lest he should take Gavin's name and the number of the Anglia also.

The detective was not impressed. He turned from me and blew a short blast on his whistle, and waved to someone unseen up the road. As though it had come straight out of an American film, a large police car appeared from nowhere and drew up diagonally across my bonnet.

I turned on the righteous indignation of the innocent citizen whose liberty is being infringed by the state.

'I've read Dicey,' I said. 'I've read Bagehot. I've even read Blackstone and the Road Traffic Acts. And not one of them says that the citizen must know the number of the car he's driving.'

At this recital of the English classicists the policeman became more polite and more insistent. Kay at this moment came out of the hotel, and began confirming everything I said. She looked as though she were ready to leap forward and bite the detective on the leg if he were not very careful.

At last I saw that our arguments were making him exasperated. We wanted at all costs to avoid being run in on suspicion of car theft. Even if we could prove our innocence of that charge, there was the jemmy in my pocket, and a torn padlock at Westminster which would set people thinking.

'Look here,' I said. 'There's a man sitting round the corner in a Ford Anglia car who can prove everything I'm saying. He's got the car hire receipt. Go and see him.'

The detective's lip seemed to curl. He thought this was a clumsy subterfuge to get him off the scene, while we made off. Yet something in our bearing made him hesitate.

'All right,' he said at last. 'But your friend can come with me.'

He took Alan round as surety, and Kay climbed in beside me. The driver of the police car eyed me distastefully, but he turned away long enough for me to slide the jemmy out of my pocket and under the seat.

In a moment the detective arrived back in affable conversation with Gavin. He had seen the car hire receipt. It was in Gavin's name, and I, uninsured as I was, had really no right to be driving the car, but the detective was quite satisfied.

He compared the receipt with the number of the car he had written down in his little black book.

'I hope you're satisfied, constable,' I said sententiously. 'You nearly made a terrible mistake.'

He apologised again and again. There were, it appeared, many dishonest people about, and one had to do one's duty. He asked us where we were going, and as that was a question we could hardly answer, we vaguely mentioned the Edgware Road as our most rapid route north. He was now bursting with the desire to be of assistance, so he directed us there with a plethora of detail.

As we drove away we suddenly relaxed. To my astonishment, I discovered that I had enjoyed every minute of the excitement. This was something nearer to honourable fight than the ignoble brush with the night watchman, when I had lied like a petty criminal held by the ear.

But in spite of our elation as we drove away, we could not avoid a feeling of unreality. It was as though we had been picked up, put on a chess-board and moved from square to square. With the lengthened perspective of time it seems even more unreal. It was an incident completely unrelated with anything else that had happened, or was to happen. We were certain that the suspicious hotel proprietor and the detective and his driver would immediately connect the disappearance of the Stone with our untimely leave-taking of Kay's hotel. Four young Scots in two cars were not that common. Yet not one of them did so. I do not know why not, yet I know the incident happened. When you set out on an adventure, happenings have a habit of happening to you.

Forty years on

I am still baffled as to why the detective did not put two and two together, and reach the right number. Perhaps he feared rebuke for not taking the number of the Anglia. Perhaps he never thought.

He was the soul of politeness. No policeman would act like that nowadays. He would run us in and ask questions afterwards. We were lucky. But at that time the police, and especially the London police, were noted for their wonderful politeness, and English justice was the envy of the world. He could be faulted for being over polite, and over credulous, but I do not agree. Nowadays they act out the fantasies they see on television and are no longer thought wonderful. Neither is English justice.

Chapter Eleven

Ever beset by doubts I was on edge again by the time we reached the Edgware Road. It was all a complicated trap, and they were following us about, laughing and waiting to pounce. But it was Kay who laughed, ridiculing any such idea, and at the Edgware Road we turned south, back towards the Abbey. I briefly explained what we now intended and asked if she was fit to go on. She assured me she was. I emphasised that it was a long time until dawn, and that it would be a long day after that, but her teeth flashed in a dark snarl, so I let it go. Her few hours in bed seemed to have done her good, and she was prepared for anything.

Only later did it come to me that yon was never flu. We had chilled her to the marrow. Then we three had stolen the excitement, while we left her sitting all day in a car, alone and waiting for action. When it did not come, her adrenalin ran out on her, and I was too selfish to notice. A kind word was all she needed, and I gave her none. She had always plenty for me, and in her need I failed her. Now, impelled by her enthusiasm and spirit, we went on for our next attempt.

We passed Marble Arch, drove down Park Lane and along Piccadilly to the Circus, which was peopled with strange figures. There are many ways of celebrating Christmas. The streets were quieter as we went west, and Whitehall was long and oily dark and empty. The only traffic was the occasional police car coming and going from Scotland Yard. Outside the War Office, we pulled in to the kerb, and Kay and I went into the Anglia to sit with the other two in our last council of war. I took the jemmy with me, hiding it under my coat. From there, I slid it under the front seat of the Anglia. We were all flushed with past excitement, and even I was eager for more, all doubts gone. Although we had been delayed, the timing was still synchronised with our calculations. Four o'clock rang from Big Ben. If our estimations were correct, the watchman should have finished his rounds.

Since the detective had taken my name and address and the number of the car I was driving, we decided to use the Anglia for the whole job. The Anglia was unknown to the police, and even if it were spotted in suspicious circumstances outside the Abbey, it was a common brand of car, and had a chance of slipping through. It would take the police some time to do all the routine work to connect us to it. We reckoned that we had a good twelve hours, and maybe more before that happened. Strangely, it was a connection they never made. It was unfortunate that we had now only one effective car, but we had to accept that. We decided also, that since I had had my name taken by the police, I would set out west for Wales in the identified car as a decoy, while the others headed south-west for Dartmoor with the Stone.

Having agreed our strategy, we moved. I parked my car in the car park along Millbank from the Abbey, and carefully locked it, and put the keys in my overcoat pocket. The detective had said there were thieves about, and I was prepared to believe him. I would need the car later. When I had secured it, I rejoined the others in the Anglia.

Old Palace Yard was deserted, so we did not need to make a dummy run. Alan swung the Anglia straight into the lane, and, halfway up, switched out the lights. At the top he manoeuvred it round skilfully in the restricted space. The engine reverberated terrifyingly off the Abbey walls, for the Ford was a noisy little car, but when it was turned, with its bonnet pointing into the lane, it seemed so small beside the soaring buttresses that we were certain it would not be seen. We got out and Kay slipped into the driving seat.

Ignoring the long way round through the mason's yard, the three of us vaulted the high railings, crossed past the lamp-post, and stood crucified by its light against the shining door. At least we should not work in darkness.

Gavin put his shoulder to the door. 'The jemmy,' he hissed.

I turned to Alan.

'The jemmy!'

'What?' said Alan. 'I thought you had it.'

Sheepishly, I returned to the Anglia and got it from under the seat where I had hidden it ten minutes before.

At first we made little impression on the door. The two halves met closely, and were covered with a lath of wood, which ran all the way over the join from top to bottom. But I knew that this was the one door in the Abbey which was of pine, and not of oak as the others were. It should be forcible. We were desperately afraid of noise, and each creak sounded like a hammer blow. Inside the Abbey it must have resounded loudly enough to awaken the many dead. You could hear them stirring and sitting up. We ignored the noise and worked on. First we prised off the covering lath of wood, and then with the sharp end of the jemmy we chewed away a sufficient space to allow us to force the blade between the two sections of the door. Then the three of us put our weight on the end of the jemmy, and the door began to give a series of creaks, each of which sounded like the report of a shotgun. At each creak we expected a police car to sweep up the lane, summoned by the watchman. Let it come. We had already done more than most.

I could now put my fingers through and feel the hasp on the inside. It was slack. One side of the door was held by a bolt mating with a hole in the stone of the floor, and when we prised up this side of the door, the bolt came free. Our gap widened to three inches. We could see into the Abbey. There was no watchman there.

We put the blade of the jemmy close behind the padlock, and together we all wrenched mightily. With a crash the door flew open. In the car, Kay heard the noise and shuddered. But the way into the Abbey was open.

We swept into the dark of the bare stone transept. I returned and pulled the doors close behind me. I had rehearsed that part.

A light glowed dimly at the west end of the nave, but the rest was in black darkness. We went down the transept in silent hurry, and found that the gate in the metal grill was open. We crept through and round and up into the Confessor's Chapel. We did not listen for the watchman, for we might have heard him coming. At least, at least, we would touch the Stone.

The chapel was in darkness. The glimmer from my torch showed the glass doors into the Sanctuary as black sheets, and I hastily turned it to the side, where it shone wanly on the green marble tomb of Edward I, whose dead bones Bruce had feared more than he feared any living Englishman.

The other two had already lifted aside the rail which kept the public back. The Stone was before us, breast high, in an aperture under the seat of the Coronation Chair. We prised at the bar of wood which ran along the front of the Chair as a retainer for the Stone. It was dry with age and it cracked and splintered. I shall strike no attitudes about being sorry to damage it. The Stone was behind it and it had to go.

The Stone should now theoretically have slipped out, but it was a very close fit and its weight made it unwieldy. I got to the back and pushed and it moved a little. The chains on the side kept catching on the carved sides of the Chair, and since the three of us were working in a sweating fever, not one of us had the patience to hold the light. At last we saw that brute strength and black darkness would not budge it, so we called a halt. Then, one man holding the torch, one prising at the sides with the jemmy, and one pushing at the back, we started afresh. It moved. It slid forward. The English Chair would hold it no longer.

We were sweating and panting. It was coming. The plaque saying "Coronation Chair and Stone" fell from the Chair. I caught it in mid air and thrust it into my coat pocket. They would not need that now. It was almost free. One last heave. 'Now,' said Gavin. I pushed from the back. It slid forward, and they had it between them. I rushed forward to help them and we staggered a yard. We had to put it down. It was too heavy.

'A coat,' said Alan deep in his throat.

'Mine is the strongest,' I said. It was the strongest, but I wanted my coat to be the one that was used. I slipped the jemmy out of my pocket. We would come back for that later. I struggled out of my coat and laid it on the ground; one hasty heave and the Stone was on the coat.

I seized one of the iron rings and pulled strongly. It came easily—too easily for its weight. 'Stop,' I said and shone my torch. What I saw astonished me, and for a moment I could not think what had happened. There was not one Stone but two. I had pulled a whole neat corner away, and it lay separate from the rest of the Stone, a gigantic cube, about one quarter of the whole.

Of course, I should have been appalled, but I wasn't. What the penalties were for breaking the Crown's Regalia I neither knew nor cared. As a unit the Stone was nearly unmanageable; as two, it made our job easier. These were my thoughts then and they still are, although I was later to conceal them with much pious humbug, pretending to have been shocked and awestruck, when I was only relieved. I picked up the small part, small but still an armful which made me stagger, and opened the door to the Sacrarium with my shoulder and passed through. The light still burned at the far end of the nave, but it only accentuated the soaring darkness of the building. Of the watchman there was no sign.

Although I must have been carrying a hundred pounds in my arms, nearly three quarters of my own weight, I ran light footed with my burden. Adrenalin is a great drug. I came out into the light outside the Poets' Corner door, and plunged into the darkness of the mason's yard, shouldering open the doors we had very wisely forced some hours before. Kay had seen me coming and had the car halfway down the lane. She opened the car door, and I rolled the piece of Stone onto the back seat.

'We've broke it,' I said, with unholy joy, lapsing into the language of my childhood. 'Get back into cover.' I don't know what she thought, but by the time I was back into the Abbey the car was once more in position at the top of the lane.

The other two had made good progress. The steps leading down from the altar are wide and shallow, and they presented little difficulty to us. We grasped the coat between us, and swung it down step by step. Except for gasps for breath, and an occasional grunt of effort, we made little noise. Now and again there was a rending sound from the coat as the weight told on it, but my father sold only the best of cloth, and it stood up to the end.

We reached the foot of the steps and dragged it on across the nave. Sweat blinded us and we were breathless. As we turned into the transept there was a crunching noise. The plaque, which I had forgotten was still in the coat pocket, had fallen out, and the whole weight of the Stone had passed over it. Alan swiftly pocketed it. That simple action was later to give me a clue that saved the whole enterprise.

Suddenly and miraculously we were at Poets' Corner door. We stopped for a breather for we were winded by the excitement as well as by our efforts. 'One more pull,' said Alan. 'We're not going to be beaten now.'

I opened the door to the lane, and as I did so I heard the car start up. It moved forward down the lane where it was clearly visible from the road. We still had to manhandle the Stone down the masons' yard. It was too early to move forward yet. 'The fool,' I said, and dashed through the line of sheds to tell Kay to get back into cover.

The car was standing outside the door in the hoarding. I opened the near side door. 'Get the car back,' I said. 'We're not ready yet.'

Kay looked at me coolly. 'A policeman has seen me,' she said. 'He's coming across the road.'

Forty years on
This is no time for comment.

Chapter Twelve

There are times in life when one leaps forward to meet whatever is coming with a joy beyond expression. It amounts to an acceptance of challenge with the certainty of success. Failure is not thought of, and each fractioned second is lived with distilled intensity. This was one of these times. We had surmounted so many difficulties that nothing could dismay us. We were caught, but we were still fighting. Part of the Stone was lying there on the back seat for anyone to see, and we had a policeman coming towards us, yet it did not occur to either of us that this was the end. This was only one more incident in a long chain of incidents. We would cope.

I got into the car and silently closed the door. I reached forward and switched on the side lights. Then I took deep breaths to steady myself and wiped the Abbey dust off my hands onto Kay's jacket. I put one hand over the back of the seat and draped Alan's spare coat over the fragment of the Stone. Then I took her in my arms.

It was a strange situation in which we found ourselves, yet neither of us felt perturbed. Kay was as cool and calm as though we were on our way home from a dance. It was our third night without sleep and I think that our tiredness helped. Certainly my heart did not race with panic, and I don't think Kay's did either. We were getting immune to adrenalin, or else our bodies had none left to give. Kay set me an example in her relaxed remoteness. She is a most remarkable woman. We cuddled one another and waited.

The policeman loomed in front of us. We could have predicted his first words.

'What's going on here?' he asked.

What appeared to be going on was apparent to everyone. Kay and I did not fall apart until he had had plenty of opportunity to observe us.

'It's Christmas Eve, you know, officer,' I explained.

'Christmas Eve, be damned!' he thundered. 'It's five o'clock on Christmas morning.'

'Ochone. Ochone,' said Kay, looking up at him with an assumed innocence that would have delighted anyone except a Wee Free Minister. 'Is it that time already?'

'You're on private property here,' he told us severely. 'And why did you move forward when you saw me coming?'

'I know,' I said humbly. 'I knew we shouldn't be here. We put on the lights to show you that we were quite willing to move on.'

'But where can we go?' asked Kay, voicing the eternal question of two youngsters, caught in the sin of being alone together. 'The streets are far too busy.'

'You should be off home," he said severely, but beyond his sternness his voice was tender, as he looked down at her loveliness.

'She's my sister,' I was about to say, eager to curry favour, and nearly blowing the whole ploy in three words. 'We're from Scotland,' I said instead, and explained that we were on holiday and that we had arrived in London too late to get a bed. We had toured round instead, looking at the lights, and had ended up here to pass the night away. We sat and held hands shamelessly in front of him, and tried to give him the impression that we were a nice couple, too much in love to go to a hotel and be parted.

He began to warm to us. To my horror he took off his helmet and laid it on the roof of the car. He lit a cigarette, and showed every sign of staying until he had smoked it.

'There's a car park just along the road,' he said helpfully. We knew that car park. The other car was there.

'Och well,' said Kay, putting her head into the lion's mouth. 'If we're not comfortable there we can always get you to run us in and give us a bed in the cells.'

'No. No,' said the policeman knowingly. 'There's not a policeman in London would arrest you tonight. None of us want to appear in Court on Boxing Day to give evidence against you.'

Kay gave my hand a squeeze. 'A good night for crime,' I said, and we all laughed.

All this time I had been conscious of a scraping sound coming from behind the hoarding. Why on earth didn't they lie low until the policeman had gone? It transpired afterwards that they had no idea that we were entertaining the police, and they were grunting away with the Stone, and calling my parentage in question for sitting in the car talking to Kay while they did all the work.

Kay heard the noise too, and we engaged the constable in furious conversation. He thought us excellent company. His slightest sally brought forth peals of laughter, and when he made a joke we nearly had convulsions. Surely they would hear our laughter and be warned. They had. They thought we had gone off our heads with the strain.

At last there was a muffled thud from behind the hoarding. The constable stopped speaking, tense, intent, listening. My heart thudded, and I swallowed a dry tongue. Kay's hand became rigid in mine. Then the constable laughed and said, 'That was the old watchman falling down the stairs,' and Kay and I laughed also; loudly we laughed at the idea of an old man falling down stairs. Surely they would hear us now.

'I wish it was six o'clock,' said the policeman, 'and then I would be off duty.'

Out of the corner of my eye I saw the door of the hoarding slowly opening. Gavin's face appeared, followed by his head and shoulders. Suddenly he froze. He had seen the policeman. Inch by inch he edged back, and inch by inch the door closed behind him. The policeman finished his cigarette, and put on his helmet. 'You'd better be going now,' he said.

'We had,' I said, trying to keep the fervour out of my voice.

'Will you show us the way?' Kay asked, trying to get him off the premises.

'Oh, you can't miss the car park,' he said, and redirected us.

Kay started the engine, and drove us off down the lane, leaving the policeman behind us. He had not asked for her licence, nor for any form of identification from me. He had asked for no papers of any kind. So far as we knew, he had not noted the car number, but it was too much to expect that he had not memorised it, or at least some of it. And some of it would be enough, for there were not many cars on the road at that time of the morning, and later on Christmas Day the roads would not be busy. Christmas was a time for home keeping. We reached Old Palace Yard, and Kay put her toe down.

As she drove, I reflected on what to do next. We had won away with part of the Stone, and even part of it was success. It was enough to make our point. We could not be expected to do more, and if we could get this part home it was more than anyone had done before us. A quick bolt to hide this bit somewhere, seemed to be the sensible thing to do. No one could blame us for calling it quits.

Yet quits it was not. The greater part of the Stone still lay with our two friends in the mason's yard. Somehow we must get back, and collect it, and get it into hiding. Meanwhile, the Anglia was a dangerous car. Both cars were dangerous, but of the two, the Anglia was the one more closely connected with the Abbey. As soon as the hue and cry was raised it would be stopped and its driver arrested. Ungallant as it was, Kay would have to be the one to take the greater risk, and go on with the Anglia, while I went back to the Abbey to try to get the larger part of the Stone.

As she pulled the car into the car park, it became apparent that risk was a consideration that did not weigh at all with Kay. Going on alone was no job at all for anyone, because in that car it meant almost certain arrest, and with the bit of the Stone in the back, it would be a situation which no amount of talking would explain. However, it was the best we could do, and my thoughts were already turning back to the Abbey, where we had left Gavin and Alan, and our friend the policeman. Kay had a friend in the Midlands, and she was sure that she would help her. We were clutching at straws. Bales and bales of it, had we but known, for every Scot in the world was with us, but there was no one there to tell us.

The job was half done, and it had to be finished. The policeman had said that he went off duty at six o'clock, and from his casual conversation I rather thought that he would spend the last half hour of his shift smoking in one of the police boxes which were dotted here and there about the great cities for the police to take rest periods in. If I delayed, there was less chance of meeting him again with the other car in the same lane. But I had to strike a balance. Very shortly the night watchman would go on his rounds, and discover that the Stone was missing. I would have to slot myself in before that. There was just time to put Kay on to the road to Victoria, and it would be quicker if I were to lead her there in the other car. I knew London better than she did, and once I had set her on her way I could drive back to the Abbey and pick up the other part of the Stone. It would be as simple as that. I got out of the Anglia, and felt through my pockets for the keys to other car.

Car keys are a curse. They keep more owners out of cars than they do thieves. I hunted through all the pockets in my jacket, and then through my trouser pockets, and then back to my jacket again, and then to my horror I remembered that I had put the keys safely into my coat pocket which I had taken off in the Abbey as a sledge for the Stone. The keys would still be with the two boys there. If I were to help Kay and get back to the Abbey in time, I would have to run.

First I put on Alan's old coat, which I had so recently and in such desperate circumstances laid over the bit of the Stone to cover it from the eye of the policeman. The coat fitted me more or less, though there was a shortage of buttons down the front. It was a rough disguise, for when we had talked to the policeman I had been coatless. Then I lifted the bit of the Stone into the boot, where it would be less conspicuous. All this was accomplished in a few seconds, and without another backward glance, we drove out of the car park and into the maze of side streets beside the Abbey. At length we came to a set of traffic lights. This, I was certain, was Victoria. I stopped the car and got out.

'You're on your own from now on,' I said. 'Go that way,' and for the benefit of a passer-by, I kissed her on the cheek. 'It's been a lovely party, darling,' I added. Her eyes flashed appreciation of the irony, and she drove off.

She told me later that she had only driven five hundred yards before she had to stop again at traffic lights. As she pulled away, the lid of the boot flew open and her part of the Stone fell out onto the road. She stopped and lifted something approaching her own weight back into the boot, and drove off again, and reached safety.

I'm not proud of everything I did that night. First of all losing the car keys, and then not fastening the car boot, for any sake! I very nearly bungled it all. But Kay came through the whole adventure as a person of utter courage and calm, without blemish whatsoever.

Forty years on
I have been fortunate all my years. There have been many times when life has been lived with an incandescent intensity. This was now one of them.

Chapter Thirteen

Kay's departure left me standing in that London street, but I did not feel alone. Abbey fever had me in its grip again, and I started to run. Then I slowed to a walk, for a running man in an empty street arouses suspicion, and I had far too much to do to wish to cause another incident. As I hurried with all the slowness at my command, I glanced at my watch and discovered it was no longer on my wrist. Later I found out that it had burst away when I had been tugging at the Stone in the Abbey. It had been a present to my father when he retired as Session Clerk of our local Church of Scotland, and it was to remain one of the great unsolved clues left for the police.

Clue for the police it was, but it left me only with my own estimate of time, and things were getting very tight. At first I was not sure where I was, but my frequent reconnaissance now stood me in good stead, and soon I found myself in familiar surroundings. I hoped that Kay was not too lost. Near the Square I passed a policeman. I kept my head well down lest it was our friend. If it was, then the coat was a good disguise, for he went his way, longing no doubt for six o'clock, and dreaming of promotion. A little quiver of compassion shot through me for the unfortunate fellow. He would have a lot of explaining to do to his superiors.

I circled the Abbey. When I came to the East side, I slowed to a troubled stroll. Everything was unnaturally quiet. I could scarcely believe it. It was either a trap or another chance, and if it was a chance I was willing to take it. As I rounded the snub nose of Henry VII's Chapel there was no one in sight, so I swung straight into the lane, and passed through the door into the mason's yard.

There was no one there. The place was in black darkness. I stood for a moment stock still, listening to the utter silence. Even the sounds of the night had gone. The Stone lay at my feet. I could feel it, but of Alan and Gavin there was no sign. They must be in hiding.

'Alan! Gavin!" I called in a whisper.

The whole night seemed to quiver with my voice, but not an echo replied. Fear ran a feather over my hair.

I shook myself and moved up through the dark sheds. They might be in hiding in the Abbey. I eased open the door to Poets' Corner, and went in. The light still glowed at the far end of the nave. I risked a breathless whistle. There was no response.

I retraced my steps and looked for my coat. I searched in the dark for it, but I could not find it. My coat and my two friends had been swallowed up by the night. This time I was not only alone. I was unutterably lonely.

It came to me in a rush, and I was out of the yard, closing the door behind me. I swung into Old Palace Yard, and exchanged a bluff Merry Christmas with an early riser. As soon as he was out of sight, I broke into a trot. The other two would be waiting for me in the car park.

I reached the car park. The old Ford was still there, dirty as ever, but no human being was in sight. As I lacked the knowledge to start it without the key, it was so much junk. I was new to cars. I sat on the wing of the car and lit a cigarette. There was nothing more I could do. At such times you don't philosophise. I don't anyway. I can scarcely think. Yet I thought a little, and felt pretty bitter about it all. Success had been ours and we had failed to grasp it. We had got the Stone to the very edge of freedom, and Luck, which had flowed so generously towards us, had started to ebb. I drew the smoke and it tasted like sand. We would be laughed at in Scotland and jailed in England, and we deserved to be, for we had been beaten.

I threw away my cigarette and broke into a run back to the Abbey. This time I was not worried about being conspicuous. There was no time for that. The chance was so slim that I was a fool to try it, yet in my mind there had been such faith that I did not for a moment think that success would elude us.

As I ran I thought. The keys of the car had been in my coat pocket. Presumably Alan and Gavin had looked for the keys in the coat pocket and had not found them. If they had, they would have taken the car. The car was still there. Therefore Alan and Gavin did not have the keys. The plaque which I had put in my pocket had been pulled out when we were dragging the Stone. Perhaps the keys had fallen out also. Perhaps if I went back into the Abbey and searched I would find them. Perhaps. I reached the Abbey and went in for the fourth time that night.

I had left my torch with Kay, so I was sightless. On my hands and knees I groped along the route we had taken until I reached the altar steps. Then I remembered my matches and by the flickering light of a match held in my hand, I retraced my steps. In that vast darkness the light lit nothing but myself, but I persisted until the matchbox was nearly empty. Suddenly near the door I put my foot on something uneven. I bent down and picked up the keys. The ring had been flattened by the passage of a heavy weight, but the keys were undamaged.

I ran back all the way to the car. If my calculations of time were correct, the night watchman would be starting his rounds any time now. The car battery was flat, but I took out the starting-handle and swung the engine over by hand. In spite of the cold it started on the first pull. I raced the engine furiously to warm it, for I did not dare to have it stall on me and not restart. I'd have given up then. I pulled out of the car park, and along into Old Palace Yard. There were two policemen at the door to the Houses of Parliament under St. Stephen's Tower. Things were waking up, and already there were some pedestrians around, but I had to take my chance. The night watchman would start his rounds at any time now. I did not know the time, but I knew it was running out for me. I swung the car boldly into the lane in full sight of the policemen.

In the lane I did not bother to switch off the car lights, for subterfuge was now useless. I backed up as fast as I could, and in my excitement smacked the hoarding heavily with the wing of the car. I had no very clear idea of what I was going to do, except that I was going to get the Stone into the car, and drive away with it. Sometimes life's that simple.

The Stone was still lying where the other two had left it. I caught hold of it by one end and dragged it to the car. I do not recall having any difficulty. I raised it up on its good end so that it stood near the car, and then I walked it, corner by rocking corner, to the car door and tipped one end in. The car came down with a crash onto its springs, and I thought for a moment it was going to beetle over on top of me. I got hold of the end that was still on the ground and lifted it mightily until it passed top dead centre, when it fell, with another fearful crash, into the car. I followed it in, and lifted it bodily onto the back seat. Then I took off Alan's coat and covered it up and went back into the driving seat and drove away down the lane.

I drove down the lane as Andrew Hyslop, the night watchman was telephoning the police to report his loss. I did not know that then, but it would have made no difference to me.

I was a young man. We had so very, very nearly been defeated on so many occasions, but we had persisted. It was a lovely victory, but I was too elated to be proud. That would come later, and it has never left me. I shouted and sang. Let them take me now and all Scotland would be at my back, not that I cared then, and I still don't care. I never have. A nation's soul is in its people's keeping. In the keeping of each one of us, day and daily, wherever we are, and whatever we do. For an instant that morning I felt that it was in mine alone. I hoped that Kay would feel the same.

I drove through Parliament Square, and swung round the roundabout and across the bellmouth of Whitehall, past the tower of Big Ben, which I had never noticed striking all that hectic night and morning, then I was on Westminster Bridge and south of the river. I reckoned that I had at best an hour and a half before the police could get their forces mustered. I was certain that they would be stupid enough to concentrate their forces on the roads to the North. It was Christmas Day, and they would be bleary with sleep. Still, I could take no chances. I was on my own. I must find the first piece of open ground, and hide the Stone.

The trouble was that I did not know the road. This had not been part of the plan. I knew that I should find the Old Kent Road, and by good luck I hit it quite quickly. But I could not keep to it. Perhaps it was not adequately signposted, or perhaps I was stupid from lack of sleep, but at any rate I lost my way and wandered around in a maze of side streets. I asked and was directed, or misdirected. Every village has its idiot, and I spoke to all of them in London in that short drive. A cold grey dawn was beginning to creep up the Thames from the sea, and I was almost in tears of frustration. To have the most valuable cargo that had ever entered a car, and to be the most sought after man in Britain were two responsibilities I could bear. But to be lost nearly ended me. I was driving desperately down a mean street when another of the coincidences happened which were to mark the whole course of our enterprise. There, plodding away from me, were the familiar figures of Alan and Gavin.

We had never been in this part of the city before. They were walking without design, and I was driving in a maze, completely lost. It was a plain miracle, and it did not even surprise me.

I drove fast, and pulled up wickedly behind them with a squeal of brakes. It was a rotten thing to do, and would have frightened the wits out of me if someone had done the same to me. Without a glance behind them they broke and fled precipitately down the street. The weight of their consciences drove them on. Running and guilt are close companions. I laughed like the bastard I am. The street was deserted. I stopped and shouted out the open window at them.

'I've got a bit of Bannockburn in the back seat.'

At that they stopped running and came back. I opened the near side door.

'I've got it. I've got it,' I said. 'Look! It's in there.'

They thought I was talking about the small piece, until I pulled back the coat and showed its rough loveliness to their delighted eyes. Then they both dived to get in beside it, and jammed in the door.

'Only one,' I said. It was an old car and I was afraid for the springs. Alan fell inside, and Gavin closed the door.

'Meet at Reading Station at four o'clock,' we agreed. Then we shared our money out to see that none of us would go wanting. I let in the clutch, and we left Gavin standing on the pavement, looking as though we had marooned him.

We swung from mean street to mean street, and had to ask our way several times. We were still lost but our reunion had heartened us. I had been worried about man-handling the Stone out of the car into hiding by myself, but what would almost have been an impossibility for one was easy for two. Finally, somewhere about Shooters Hill, we hit the Rochester Road. Exhausted and light hearted with victory I handed over the wheel to Alan. He put his toe down and we raced into the south.

"We did it. We did it.' A hundred times I told him all that had happened to me since I had left them in the Abbey to see why Kay had moved the car forward. He listened to me gently, like the great quiet gentleman he is.

Then, as we crossed Eltham Common and plunged into suburbia, it was Alan's turn to talk. When he and Gavin had noticed the policeman they had faded into the shadows, certain that at any moment they would see the door swing open as he came to investigate. When they heard Kay and me drive away they waited a few minutes and then crept down the lane almost on the heels of the policeman, bringing my coat with them. They reached the car park just as Kay and I were driving away in the Anglia, and although they ran after us, they were too late to stop us. They immediately searched for the keys of the other car in my coat pocket, and not finding them assumed that I had them with me. Just then a police car had raced along Millbank towards the Abbey, its siren going, and thinking the game was up, they had started to walk aimlessly, until, by the grace of God, I had almost run them down.

'What happened to my coat?' I asked.

Alan looked round anxiously. 'Didn't you get it?' he asked. 'We left it behind the car.'

That was a blow, for my name was on it, and it would be discovered when the car park attendant came on duty. I thought ruefully that we had got the Stone away, but that at the same time we had left behind us a complete case for the prosecution. It was a fair exchange, and no one in our position would have grumbled.

Forty years on

It was not my finest hour. I have had finer and more private ones. Indeed I look back on that young man as a stranger. But I am still intensely and privately proud that he was me.

Chapter Fourteen

I lay back and closed my eyes and tried to relax, but I could not. Every few seconds I would sit up and try to annoy Alan by urging him on to greater speed, but he was honed to a fineness, and would not be annoyed. Then I would fret and peer in all directions, looking for a suitable hiding place for the Stone.

Suddenly I noticed that I was cold and clammy. The blood drained from my head and everything became gray. A white sweat broke out on my forehead, and I started to shudder and shake uncontrollably. I had a stiffness across the small of my back and my limbs ached. Had 1 been holding anything it would have fallen from my shaking hands. I glanced at them as they jerked sideways from the ends of my wrists as though trying to shake my fingers loose. They were scratched and worn from contact with the Stone, and although this sight steadied me a little, I was still on the point of fainting. Spots of light danced behind my eyes. I looked across at Alan, who was driving coolly, and took an enormous grasp of my self control; then I asked him if I could take the wheel, and in the excitement of driving fast on a doubtful surface the nausea passed away, and did not trouble me again.

About half past eight we sped down hill, and turning right, came to a cross roads. On the far side was a large roadhouse, built in mock Elizabethan style, and straight ahead was an avenue of poplars. We were now in open country, and two miles further on we saw a little cart track climbing into the fields. We turned the car into it and put its nose to the hill. It was a steep pull for such a little car, with such a heavy load. It whined and sang, and in the lowest of its three gears it only just made it. We had been asking a lot of it and it gave it. When we had gone fifty yards we were out of sight of the road, so we stopped the car as best we could. The brakes would not hold on the hill and we had to leave it in gear and chock one of the wheels with a boulder. Then we looked round us for a hiding place.

The Coronation Chair with the Stone of Destiny in situ. *(Outram Picture Archives, Glasgow)*

Gavin Vernon leaves Police Headquarters after a morning interview, 20th March, 1951. *(Outram Picture Archives, Glasgow)*

Gavin Vernon, Ian Hamilton and Alan Stuart. *(Outram Picture Archives, Glasgow)*

Ian Hamilton, addressing the crowd at a mass demonstration held by the Scottish Covenant Association at St. Andrew's Hall, Glasgow. 17th April, 1951. *(Outram Picture Archives, Glasgow)*

Ian Hamilton, 20th March 1951. (*Outram Picture Archives, Glasgow*)

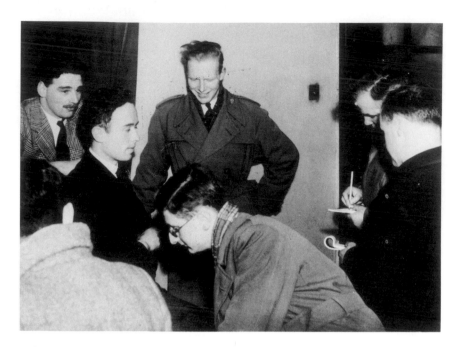

Gavin Vernon, Ian Hamilton and Alan Stuart with pressmen.
(*Outram Picture Archives, Glasgow*)

Ian Hamilton, the late John MacCormick and Gavin Vernon. 20th April, 1951. (*Outram Picture Archives, Glasgow*)

Ian Hamilton with the Petition for a Scottish Parliament. *(Outram Picture Archives, Glasgow)*

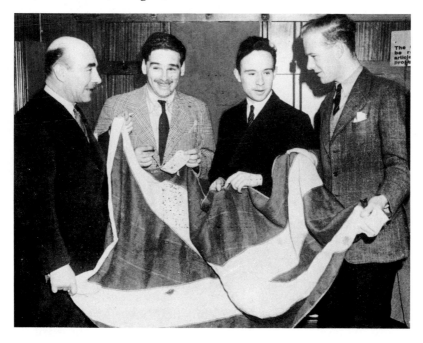

Bertie Gray, Gavin Vernon, Ian Hamilton, Alan Stuart – holding the national flag. *(Outram Picture Archives, Glasgow)*

Mr Wishart, Custodian of Arbroath Abbey (Ministry of Works)
with the Stone of Destiny on the day of its return in April, 1951.
(*Outram Picture Archives, Glasgow*)

The police carrying away the Stone of Destiny after its return, April 1951. *(Outram Picture Archives, Glasgow)*

The police guard Westminster Abbey as the Stone of Destiny is returned, 13th April, 1951. *(The Press Association)*

There was nowhere suitable in sight; the ditches were shallow hollows and the hedges, although high and straggly, were sparse and thin with winter deadness. We climbed ten feet up a grassy bank and looked down the other side into a hollow, dotted with undernourished trees. A narrow path wound through it, but it was overgrown with dead grass, and looked little used. It was far from being an ideal hiding place, but we had little choice.

Sweating and straining, we lifted the Stone from the car and half dragged, half rolled it up the bank. We were both very tired, and there was no immediate fear and excitement to spur us on. The brightness of flashing stars behind my eyeballs impaired my vision, and I found the strength gone from my fingers. We stopped frequently for a rest, and once I thought of the joy of lying down in the dirty snow and going to sleep. Then we started again, confident that one more effort would see the job done.

At length we got it to the top of the slope and let it toboggan down the other side, then we dragged it off the path among the grey rotting grass to where a few sprays of bramble had survived the winter. We threw some grass on it, and crowned it with a ragged edge of scrap metal, but it was too large to be hidden. We looked back at it from the top of the rise, and it stood out like a wart on a girl's face. We had no alternative but to leave it. Our car was too hot. The police had its number. We consoled ourselves with the thought that there were no newspapers on Christmas Day, and that even if the local people saw it they would not know what it was until they saw its description in the Press.

We backed the car onto the road and headed north for London. Now was the time for song, but we could not sing. Fatigue had its knee in our backs, and reaction was setting in. All was dullness. We turned to consider the problems, expecting at any moment to be stopped by the police. But nothing happened.

As we drove, we evolved a plan to meet the new circumstances. We had arranged to meet Gavin at Reading that afternoon, and as yet there was no reason to deduce that either he or Alan were suspected by the police. They had my name and address, and the number of our car. Since my meeting with the watchman in the Abbey, my duel with the detective outside Kay's hotel, and our conversation with the constable in the lane, I was too dangerous to be allowed near the Stone. It seemed that the best thing Alan and I could do would be to part company. Alan would meet Gavin at Reading, and together they would hire a car and transport the Stone to Dartmoor, while I would play the old game of decoy, and make for Wales in the Ford.

However, we could do nothing until we got to London. The thought of my coat was festering away in my mind. Unless the police had found it, it was still lying in the car park beside the Abbey. While we felt that we had left so many clues behind us as to make our detection certain, we did not wish to hand the police evidence on a tray. That coat had my name on it, and the address of my father's tailor's shop. It had to be recovered.

We drove back through suburbia feeling for the residents what a deep-sea sailor must feel for a ferryman. These people who were rising to beer and turkey and to another Christmas Day had something which I should have been terrified to possess. I have always been afraid of the sameness of life in which each day is worn to a thinness, and night brings only the promise of an identical dawn. I wanted to make my life an adventure, and already I was filling it with bright things. It lacked only security, which is the cement of society, and the God of suburban life. I thought that morning that if I always sought adventure, I could go on to the end without security. Instead of a pension and a portfolio of shares, I would have a pageant in my mind of a life lived to the full. I would trade wealth for the richness of life itself, even if it meant dying a pauper. So far I've managed.

These thoughts sustained me while we drove back into town. I will never know how we managed, for we had only the vaguest idea of the route we had come. We had lost our way many times coming out, and we expected to do the same thing going back, but suddenly I realised that we had hit the Lambeth Road, and in a few minutes we were on Lambeth Bridge. We looked to our right towards the Abbey, and wondered what was happening in the Confessor's Chapel. However, when we did a dummy run past the car park there was no one about, so we stopped the car on the road opposite, and retrieved the coat. It was in a terrible state. There remained only the plaque to be found.

But the plaque could not be found. It was not a matter of great importance, but it was the only end left to us to tidy up. It was the one which said, "Coronation Chair and Stone." Without amendment it would be of no further use to the Abbey authorities. However, we could not find the bombed site where it had been hidden. Undismayed, we laughed. 'Never mind,' said Alan. 'When they find it they'll dig up every bombed site in London to try to find the Stone.' We could not foresee that it would be a month before it was found, and its discovery would give a distracted Scotland Yard something new to think about. Before that, they had dragged most stretches of water in central London. Their operations in the Serpentine attracted every Scot in London to jeer them on.

When we gave up our search I took over the wheel, for I knew London better than Alan. We headed west through Hammersmith. We drove to meet Gavin at Reading, and, although Alan ought to have gone by train in case the car should be stopped, we did not press the matter. There was a haven of comradeship in the car, and we needed each other's support.

We arrived in Reading about ten o'clock and immediately went to the station for a wash. There was no sign of Gavin, but we had not arranged to meet until four o'clock, and he had probably stayed in London for a meal. We would both have enjoyed one too, because we had not eaten since the previous night, and we were starving. But it was Christmas Day, and the town was locked and deserted, and indeed we had little money for food.

I gave most of the money I had to Alan. Money is only scraps of tokens, and has no meaning except in the artificial conditions we live in, but artificial or not we needed more. Together we could only muster about fifteen pounds. Gavin also had some, but I was afraid that even pooling their resources, he and Alan might not have enough to hire a car, so I decided to telephone Bill Craig in Glasgow, and have more sent to Gavin care of the Strand Post Office. I could not use Alan as the addressee, as no one in Glasgow knew he was with us. They would have to wait until the Post Office opened after the Christmas holiday, which was no bad thing. Having arranged these things, I drove off westwards, leaving Alan gazing after me in the station square.

It was a bright morning and the roads were deserted. The snow had gone from them, and the car and I sang to each other as we sped westwards. I wanted to put as much distance as possible between myself and Reading, for I still thought that my arrest was imminent, and I did not want the police to deduce that my accomplices might be there. Near Thatcham I found a telephone box, and put a call through to Bill Craig. There was a pause as his mother went to fetch him.

'This is Ian Johnstone.' I said excitedly when at last he came.

'Who's Ian Johnstone?' he asked. He had forgotten my code name and he sounded ill-tempered as though newly risen.

'You know Ian Johnstone,' I said. It was my turn to be ill-tempered. He had forgotten the code, and I envied him his bedroom yawn. 'Wake up,' I snarled, and at that he recognised my voice. Then I made the arrangements for the money to be sent, and at the end I added casually, 'By the way, Bill, the book has been a great success down here.' He knew what I meant at once. 'Has it?' he said, a flame in his voice, and at that I put the 'phone down without satisfying his further appetite. Let the bastard starve.

Days later I heard Bill's reactions to my cryptic message. He told me that when we left for London he had not much hope of our success. He had expected us to arrive back in Glasgow with our money spent, and the most valid reasons for our failure, as indeed we might have done, if we had given up when I was first caught by the night watchman. He had listened to the radio on Sunday, and, when there was no news from Westminster, had concluded that we had done nothing. Then came my telephone call.

His first reaction was disbelief. Then it dawned on him that I would not have spoken as I had done had we not succeeded in some measure at least. Even then he did not believe in our complete success. At best, surely, all we had done was broken into the Abbey and moved the Stone. It was beyond the most intense optimism that we had succeeded entirely. At once he telephoned John MacCormick. In carefully guarded terms he told him that I had telephoned and claimed success. I can imagine the reply in a rather cold, almost uninterested voice. 'Oh, yes, Bill.' And he would go on playing Christmas games with his children, while his mind slipped its clutch with excitement. When he could find a moment he would slip away from his family and telephone Councillor Gray.

In an hour or so the Christmas programmes on the radio were interrupted to give the news. I am told that Scotland spent one of the most excited Christmasses it had had for years. John's flat was besieged by reporters, and Councillor Gray had to fend them off as best he could. From that day onward they both answered all questions with calm irony, which, if it did not avert suspicion, gave nothing away. Thus while the police combed Britain for the criminals, the men behind the men they sought sat quietly in Glasgow and issued Press statements.

But at that time on Christmas Day we were too near the reality to be bothered with Press statements. We could not know the extent of the furore we had caused, because we had no radio, and there were no English newspapers on Christmas Day. We hoped that the interest would be great, for that was one of our intentions. The time would come when our tongues would go into our cheeks also, and we would talk and speculate and lay bets as to where the Stone was hidden, but that irony lay in the future. We still had a lot to do.

After making the telephone call I drove on west. There was a pleasure in driving on such a morning, but I began to feel that perhaps I was being over cautious in laying down a false trail. Policemen and even police stations had no radios in these days, and it took them many hours to marshall their men, and call them in from their homes, but I did not know the difficulty they were having. I did not wish to underestimate their powers of deduction, and I had worked all morning on the assumption that they would connect the four Scots and the two cars outside Kay's hotel with the disappearance of the Stone only an hour or two later. I think it was a reasonable assumption, but as I drove on I became increasingly aware that I had been passed by one or two police cars, none of which had shown the slightest interest in me. What if I were to reach Wales without the police paying any attention to me? Was I to sit there inactive and wait to be arrested? I decided that, in the absence of a police hunt, the best thing I could do was to return to Reading and help Alan and Gavin to retrieve the Stone. It was a wise decision to take. Had I continued to give the police credit for the intelligence I thought they possessed, I would have arrived helplessly in Wales, and Alan would have had the whole responsibility for removing the Stone, for Gavin never arrived in Reading.

Before turning the car and heading back the way I had come, I stopped at a little pub high on the downs above Marlborough. It was half an hour before twelve o'clock when they opened officially, but they let me in and gave me a big plate of bread and mutton, which I ate with relish, for I was starving. Their radio was in their private quarters, so I was unable to hear the news, and after drinking a bottle of beer when opening time came, I headed back the way I had come.

Alan was waiting at Reading Station when I arrived. He too had only had a sandwich, and we drove round the town looking for a hotel to give us lunch, but they were all booked for Christmas dinners, so there was no room at the inns. We had a note of the times of all the trains from London, and we met each one, our hope dwindling as we saw no sign of Gavin. We waited, cold and hungry and tired, until half past four, and then pressed the starter and headed back for London and the Stone.

It was still light when we reached London, so we went for a

wash and a meal. The job we had to do could only be done in darkness. We parked the car in a side street off Piccadilly, and went into a restaurant. We were fighting shy of Whitehall and the Strand, where we had eaten many times in the last few days. At the next table a group of two men and two women were talking loudly about the remarkable happenings in the Abbey, so we kept our Scots accents muted. Feeling like new men, we went back to the car, but before we set out for the Dover Road, we stopped at a telephone box, and I put through another call to Bill. He was jubilant.

'Never mind talking in riddles,' he said, when I started to use the cumbersome code. 'They can't be tapping every line to Scotland. There's nothing else in the papers or on the radio, except what you've done. The Border roads have road blocks on them for the first time in four hundred years, and the whole of Scotland is mad with excitement. There are two descriptions out. I can recognise them but they're not a hundred per cent. How are you standing up to it?'

'Fine,' I said. I could have listened to him all night.

'Well lie low,' he said. 'And good luck.' Then we rang off, and Alan telephoned his people. In guarded terms he explained where he was, and what he had been up to. They were astounded. They thought he had been at a wedding.

We climbed back into the car and headed for the Stone. At the back of our minds lay a worry for Gavin. His absence seemed inexplicable. We consoled ourselves with the knowledge that he must still be free. Had the police arrested him, it would have been in the Glasgow papers. The papers had been full of the Stone, but had said nothing about any arrest.

So the publicity started. It has haunted me for the rest of my life. The unco guid were tearing their raiment on both sides of the Border, for there is no one quicker to take affront at an insult to Britain than an Anglicised Scot, unless the insult comes from an Englishman. These people I had overheard at the next table in the restaurant were ordinary English people, and they were speaking in laughing delight at what had happened. They saw in it a relief from the tension of the wars and strikes and hunger and famine that daily filled the papers.

I was beginning to get the feeling that it went even further than that. Perhaps in Scotland we were reviving the spirit which has kept us the oldest unconquered nation in Europe, indeed a nation that has never known conquest. Now, more than ever, we needed to make that spirit felt at home and abroad. The nineteenth and twentieth centuries had crowded the ordinary man into a system, and labelled him, and ticketed him, and made him anonymous. We four had shown that classification had gone too far and we had burst through into the unclassified, and I hoped, the unclassifiable. In doing this I wanted to think that we had done something for England as well; for the wee ordinary men and women of the two nations. Although we are different we should also be friends. Mediocrity and acquiescence in the status quo have for too long been the ingredients of success. That is what makes you grand, pot bellied, and solemn. We had poked the pot bellies in the ribs, and made them gasp. We had done something for the wee men, because that is what we were ourselves, three wee men and a girl. While the big ones howled, and the police went into a flutter, the wee men of both nations laughed and laughed. Laughter and a pinch of salt are better than bombs any day, and we had set the world to laughter.

Forty years on
These views have never left me. Long live laughter, particularly at those who presume to govern us.

A few words of explanation about telephone calls and codes are needed. In 1950, and for many years thereafter, all long distance calls were connected by the operator at the telephone exchange. The operator could, in theory, listen in to the telephone call, although they were not supposed to do so, and, in fact, I doubt very much if it ever happened. In any event, although we had planned to use codes we were too excited to be able to stick to them. We were amateurs, not trained undercover agents, and after all, we succeeded.

Chapter Fifteen

On that day I lost my freedom. Twenty four hours earlier we could have called the whole thing off, and gone home to live with nothing worse than our private shame at our failure. Up until then, all that had driven us on had been the desire to serve, the same desire which had made me volunteer for the armed forces of the crown as a schoolboy in time of war. Now we had gone further and assumed a responsibility, and once assumed, responsibilities can never quite be shaken off. What we had done had passed from the private to the public, and we had to see the business through to the end. The temptation to run for home was a very real one, and I would never blame anyone who has the sense to run away from anything. I bolt whenever I decently can, but the Stone had to be moved, so we did not bolt. We had to put the Stone somewhere it would never be found. That was our plain duty.

As we drove south, our resolution solidified. We would pick up the Stone and hide it as quickly as possible, for we still feared that the police were looking for the car. We were fortunate to find our way without too much difficulty, and were thus able to dispose of a secret fear which we both held. It would have been irony indeed if we had been unable to locate the hiding place. However, before long we came down hill to the roadhouse, which was alive with Christmas parties. We left it behind us and drove on into the frost and cold, feeling not a bit envious, and indeed, insufferably smug, because we were living, while the party-goers were acting out a charade of festivity because the calendar told them to. When we came to our side road, we slowed down because the lights of a car shone brightly behind us. We wanted no witnesses. When the car passed we pulled up the road and switched our lights off.

It was a frosty night with only a slight threat of mist in the air. The sky was hazy with the lights of eight million people, and the nearer darkness was more intense by comparison. We prepared the car for the Stone and climbed over the fence with the fear for noise which darkness brings. People whisper at night.

The Stone was exactly where we had left it, and we set about manoeuvring it up the slope to the waiting car. The first tug on it almost broke our hearts. It seemed part of Mother Earth, yet we had moved it before, and we could move it again. The grass was slippery, and that did not make the job any easier. At one point the Stone slipped from our hands and tobogganed back down the slope. We could have cried with vexation, and I lay down for a moment forgetful of the cold and wet, tired beyond understanding. Then we attacked it again, and somehow got it up over the brow of the hill, down the slope, and into the car.

Our next job was to find a hiding place. We were somewhere in Kent, a county of which we knew little, except that hops grew there. Presumably it was open country.

We turned south and drove for twenty miles; then we cut off right, into what we hoped was open country. We drove for miles. The whole countryside was a maze of hedge-lined lanes and narrow sunken roads, which wound from sign post to sign post, and never lost sight of a house. It was suburbia in the countryside, and we began to get desperate.

A dozen times we stopped the car to look at a likely place, only to discover it was somebody's back garden. We laughed rather worriedly at the idea of hiding it in some rich stockbroker's shrubbery, and at what he would say to the police and they to him, and who would say it first. We drove on for weary miles, pulled up a steep hill, the engine complaining in first gear at the weight of the Stone, crept cautiously down the other side, and came on more and still more houses.

For half an hour Alan had been arguing that the main road was the best place. 'Hide it where they'll least expect it,' he urged, but I would not listen to him. I feared discovery by the chance passer-by. Now, however, when I saw how densely populated the district was, I knew he was right and fell into agreement with him. The problem was how to get back onto the main road, for we were hopelessly lost, and our large-scale touring map was of little use to us. At length by luck, and by diligently reading the sign posts, we found it and turned south.

In this wilderness of suburbs I was suddenly homesick. I thought of my own underpopulated country, and how easy it would be to hide an army in it. I saw the Braes up behind Paisley where I had been born, and remembered the greyness of them in winter when the south-west wind came in from Ailsa Craig, and the rain washed them and bent the rough grass flat. That was a country where a man had room to move and think without trespassing on his neighbour's garden or thinking his neighbour's thoughts. I thought of the Island of Arran, which hangs like a mirage far beyond Renfrewshire, but clear in the grey sea on a good day. I had gone there on holiday once. You could tramp over the hills all day and see nothing but the heather and the green bracken; you could watch the rain come in over the Kilbrannan Sound and wipe Goat Fell clean off the picture. I wondered of any of these men of Kent had ever seen the blush of green bracken on the throat of a hill. If they had not, I pitied them.

It was a far cry from the hills to this place and we knew it well. Half a mile down the road we stopped and looked around us. Anything was better than to drive until dawn brought arrest. It seemed to our strained nerves that to make the effort of hiding the Stone was better than to drive aimlessly. On the south side of the road was a stretch of grass, perhaps twenty paces across; beyond this was a clump of bushes in which a sparrow would have looked like an eagle. With the optimism born of fear we dragged the Stone across and thrust it into the undergrowth, only to drag it back, laughing at our folly, to fight down the fear and panic which was rising in our throats. Were we never going to come to an end?

We let in the clutch and drove east, thinking of the sea shore. A few miles further on we passed the outline of aircraft hangars on our right and shortly after came to a line of trees. Alan stopped the car and I ran over to examine the place.

It was ideal. The road at this point was ten yards out from the trees, and beyond the fence the ground sloped steeply down an embankment to a wood. The embankment was overgrown, and littered with dead leaves, windblown straw, and scraps of paper. Above all a quick scratch with my hand showed that the leaves had kept the frost from penetrating the ground, so that the earth was soft, and could easily be hollowed away to make a bed for the Stone.

I went back to Alan and again we manhandled the Stone from the car. We had almost worn away the upholstery, but that was the least of our worries. We took the map with us, and whenever a car passed, as we worked our way across the grass strip, we sat on the Stone and consulted the map, hoping that we did not look too conspicuous. Sitting in the black dark reading a map, we did not look in any way conspicuous. We looked plain daft. It was a measure of our tiredness. We dragged the Stone under the fence, and half way down the slope I hollowed a recess in the earthy mould. We lifted the Stone bodily into it, and covered it first with earth, then with leaf mould and straw, and then with papers. In the dim of the night we stood back to admire our handiwork. We were certain we had done a good job.

We returned to the car and drove on to Rochester. We were not sure exactly where we were and we wanted to get a fix on a large town. In five minutes we came to the outskirts and determined to get a meal, or a drink at least, for we were far from home, and very tired. To our surprise the pub we approached was closed. We asked a passer-by the time and he indicated the clock on a church steeple, which showed it was after midnight. Dismayed at the lateness of the hour we set off back the way we had come, but before we did so we searched the car for incriminating evidence. The iron bar to which we had hoped to lash the Stone on our first attempt was all we had left. We had wrapped it up in crepe paper to make it look like a Christmas gift if we had to carry it through the streets. We ripped the paper off it, and left it lying behind the pub. I expect it is there still.

Leaving the pub we checked the milometer on the car, and

rechecked it as we passed the spot where the Stone was hidden. We were two and a half miles distant from Rochester. Our duties ended, I lay along the back seat, and Alan put his toe down for Scotland. We had hidden the Stone where it would never be found. We alone knew where it was hidden, and we were certain that when we were arrested we could get the information out to some fellow Scot. We only hoped that Kay was as fortunate with her piece as we had been with ours.

I lay and slept for I was now very tired. It was not the ninety odd hours since we had been in bed that did it. It was the way we had passed them. They had been hectic. Now that we had discharged our responsibilities I slept like a dead man. As we approached the outskirts of London I woke up and took over. Alan, white-faced and staring, stumbled into the back seat and collapsed. Thus, one sleeping and the other driving, we passed through London. When we reached the open road we both slept in snatches, pulling into the gateway of a field for half an hour, and then one would wake, and drive on. It is a journey which is recalled only through a haze of exhaustion. Some time after dawn I wakened and looked around me. We had managed to reach the Great North Road near Biggleswade. Indeed I recognised the very spot because I had been stationed near there during my time in the Royal Air Force. We were fifty miles from London, and eighty miles from Rochester. We had taken eight hours to cover eighty miles, which broke no record. But we were on the way home.

Forty years on
The story speaks for itself, and after the passage of years I have little to add. We had no feeling of achievement at that time, nor one of anti-climax. It was a slog. We had done what we had set out to do, and our one hope was that we would get back home before the police caught up with us. Beyond all reason, Scotland seemed safe.

Chapter Sixteen

Swiftly I eased myself out into the cold greyness, and the fresh air slapped me across the face. It was a bonny morning and I felt my blood leap at the feel of it. A hoar frost had turned the grass white, and softened the brown of the ploughed fields. A morning mist hung over the fat Bedfordshire farmlands, and the sun glowed like a red ball well up in the eastern sky. I stretched and straightened myself, and the knots in my back worked loose. I was terribly glad I was alive.

I had left the door open, and the fresh air wakened Alan. He climbed out wearily, and then blinked and smiled.

'Where are we?' he asked.

'Biggleswade,' I said.

'How odd!' He seemed surprised. 'We've come a long way then.'

Since he had driven much of the way the remark shows how tired we were. We got out the map and gleefully studied the road we had come. We could remember little of it. All these miles made good seemed like a prize won in a raffle.

We washed ourselves in the roadside frost and dried ourselves on my towel, which was dirty and clammy and seemed uncivilised compared to the cleanness of the morning. Then we lit cigarettes as though the fresh air was not good enough by itself.

We looked at each other and smiled. Last night's horror of weariness had passed completely, and what for twenty four hours had seemed like a dream we now knew to be reality. We had crossed the Border and raided the very heart of Englishry, and we were returning unscathed, while all around us the authorities gnashed their teeth, and held committee meetings. Again and again we went over the details. 'Remember this! Remember this!' we cried. We recalled all the incidents, and contrasted our dejection when I had been caught by the watchman, with our present elation. There is no feeling quite like the shadowless happiness of the hour after success. We drove off shouting and singing, quite unbalanced with carelessness. We were young and triumphant, and all the glory of the morning was on our lips.

Self consciousness had parted from us long ago. We resurrected some of the old Jacobite songs and gave new meaning to them, quite unaware that in Scotland almost everyone who could sing was doing the same thing. This was something to sing about. As we passed through village after village our voices drifted out of the window, to the amazement of the stolid English pedestrians, who must have thought we were drunk. We careered up England roaring and singing.

Occasionally we fell silent and talked about Kay, who was our only worry. We had had no news since I had telephoned Bill the previous night, and we were very afraid she had been caught. She had been in the Anglia, the dangerous Anglia, which had been seen outside the Abbey. It seemed inconceivable that she could get through in such a kenspeckle car, and we hoped that she had gone to ground. It would be a hollow victory if she and her part of the Stone had been captured. We wondered, too, what had happened to Gavin, but we felt that he would be quite safe, for there was no reason to believe that he was a suspect.

Then we would fall to singing again, or I would recite 'Edinbane', one of the modern ballads of Skye, which I have repeated to myself many times since in lonely travelling. It tells about the happiness of the journey's end, and it was not inappropriate to us as we drove up England towards home.

> I will take the road right gaily,
> Heed no storm of wind or rain,
> When at journey's end there's ceilidh
> At the Inn of Edinbane.
>
> Weariness will bring no sorrow,
> I'll be younger every mile,
> When I know that ere tomorrow
> I'll be on Cuchullain's Isle.

Occasionally, when we had tired of verse or song, I would think of Bill Craig, and how he would regret for the rest of his life that he had not come with us.

In more serious moments, we talked about what we had done. The shadow of jail did not fall across our minds, and since we had seen no papers we could not tell what the general reaction was going to be. Anyone interested in history would know the reason for what we had done, but we hoped that our action might find a more general acclaim. But, in truth, we were too wrapped up in the joy of accomplishment to weigh nicely the final result.

We took turns at driving, and although the roads were treacherous we made good speed, for we knew exactly what our car would do. When we came to Stamford we stopped, and I went into the Post Office to telephone Bill for news. Alan went off to find somewhere we could get breakfast. In a short time he joined me with the grim news that everywhere was closed. It seemed that the natives were celebrating some festival called Boxing Day.

I got onto Bill almost immediately. I could sense his delight when he heard my voice. He must have had an anxious night, wondering where we were, what we were doing, and knowing that he could do nothing to help.

'How's Christmas?' I asked.

'Fine,' he said. I could hear the chuckle in his voice. My vociferous contempt and dislike for Christmas was notorious. 'There's a big party going on. One of the guests has just arrived. He's fine. We're still waiting for his partner.'

Good! That meant that Gavin was home, and that Kay was still safe.

We thought around for other double-talk to confuse any operator who might be whiling away the time by listening in, and finally realised the absurdity of the idea, and relapsed into realities.

'The Border's closed,' he said. 'Everything coming into Scotland's being searched.'

'Are the English putting up customs posts at last?' I asked innocently, and we both laughed.

112

'You'd better go to ground.'

'Not at all,' I said. It was his job to worry, and my job to refuse advice. Go to ground, indeed! We had no friends like Kay had to hide with, and could only travel on hopefully. When he saw I was adamant, he urged me again, fearing more for the Stone than for us.

'Well, for God's sake don't lose it now. If you've hidden it, send me a map.'

On this note of caution he rang off, and I reflected on what he had said. I did not wish to commit the hiding place of the Stone to paper, in case in some unknown way the police had got on to Bill. Yet it was the safest thing to do. Suppose we were captured and sent to prison without getting a chance to disclose where the Stone lay? Or worse still, suppose we were involved in an accident and both killed? These things happened. Was this great relic which had been venerated for thousands of years to pass from history because two boys had had their lives snuffed out in a skidding car? On the back of an envelope I drew a plan. I sealed it in a registered envelope and posted it to Bill at the University Union. That would be safer than his home address. Then I went back and found Alan asleep in the car.

By the time we reached Grantham we were both in need of food. More important than that, the car was beginning to show signs of the ill use it had been put to. There was three inches of play in the steering wheel, and we were not at all sure that it would not come off in our hands at any moment. We were losing power too, but I was certain that a minor adjustment would cure that.

We were too late at the George for breakfast, and too early for lunch, but they fixed us up with parsimonious tea and biscuits. Then I took off my jacket and had a look at the car. I am fond of engines, and it is one of my particular vanities that they run better when I am standing near them. They like me. Furthermore before I had left Glasgow I had bought an expensive wrench. I had hoped to use it on an Abbey door, but the occasion had not arisen.

113

Now I attacked the carburettor with it, and in a few minutes I had cured it. The steering wheel was, however, quite beyond my compass, and although I poked and pried it was only to impress Alan that I knew what I was doing. We drove off, Alan complaining witheringly that before I had put spanner to car we could have got home in twelve hours, while now we would be lucky if we got home in twenty four.

We pushed steadily on, one sleeping dreamlessly, the other shouting and singing to keep awake. We stopped for lunch at a roomy hotel called The Bell, which must have been an old coaching inn. It was civilised. We washed with soap and water and, although we were as shabby as our car, they made us welcome, as all inn folk should. There was still Christmas fare on the menu; we ate hugely, and felt that we must indeed be getting nearer home.

When we had passed through Doncaster we knew we were getting into Indian Country, and could expect police patrols. It was the middle of the afternoon before we were stopped. I was lying dozing on the back seat, when Alan, who had been silent for some time, said quietly:

'It's the police, Ian.'

I was awake immediately. We were following close on the bumper of a police car which was travelling slower and slower.

'Where are we?' I asked. Not that it mattered.

'Twenty miles north of Doncaster,' he replied.

He pulled out to pass the police car, and as we drew level the two constables scrutinised us closely. I gave them a cold incurious stare, and then we were past them. In a moment they put on speed, and were travelling beside us, signalling us to stop. They pulled in front of us and came round to Alan's window, their notebooks at the ready. We were too tired to be frightened. Arrest now or arrest in a week's time, what did it matter? Yet it would be nice to win through another adventure, and get home again.

They asked for Alan's driving licence, and as he handed it to them he said laconically, 'Not again.'

'What do you mean, *Not again?*' asked one officer.

114

'It's the third time we've been stopped in two hours,' he said, bluffing so calmly I had to look sternly at the police to hide my amusement.

'Where've you been?' asked the policeman.

'London,' replied Alan without a moment's hesitation.

'Where are you going?'

'Home,' he said in one word.

'What's the trouble?' I asked, leaning forward from the back seat.

'It's the Coronation Stone,' said one of the constables. 'You haven't seen it, have you?'

I could have laughed at the folly of the question. 'No,' I cried. 'But I've heard about it. It's a very good show. Should have been done years ago.'

The constable looked at me sourly. 'We live on one island, and some people think we should all be one people,' he said.

'Aye, maybe,' I said. 'But the Scots people don't think that, and we're the people who have the edge on you today.'

He looked at me again. I was familiar with that look from my days in the Royal Air Force. It meant, 'I could run you in so quickly that your feet won't touch the ground until you hit the back wall of a cell, but I'm not quite sure what to charge you with, so it's easier to have a quiet life.'

Without a further word he handed Alan back his driving licence, and waved us on. We could not believe our luck. It was not the end after all. For the first time we felt secure. If the detective who had taken the number of this very car outside Kay's hotel had really not handed it in to the enquiry as a suspect car to be checked out, we could bluff our way through all the road blocks south of the Tweed. We went on our way rejoicing at our good fortune.

Our way brought us to Scotch Corner, just as darkness was beginning to fall. If we cut west, the road over the high moors was likely to be badly ice bound, but it was the shortest route to Glasgow. Kay too would be travelling up the west coast, and there had been so many coincidences that we could play for another

115

and go west to meet her. However, since she might be in hiding, we rejected that, and decided to take the easy way north to Newcastle and Edinburgh. But we were still worried about her.

As we approached Newcastle, night had fallen. We had done a hundred miles in just under four hours, which was not bad going, but we had been singing less and less, and saving our energies to keep the car travelling north. Although we had not been stopped again, we had passed several dozen police cars stationed at strategic intervals all along the road. The whole police force had risen to look for a Ford Anglia, and we were afraid that she might be trying to get through. I talked wildly of giving ourselves up, in the hope that we would draw the police off and let her slip through with her piece of the Stone, but fortunately Alan's wiser counsel prevailed.

As we drove into Newcastle, a town named by an English king when he built a fortress there to keep his borders against our forefathers, I reflected that it had been of little use against us this Christmas. We were in no mood however for sustained historical reminiscences, for we were yet again starving. We drove up to the station, and had a meal in the buffet. While we were eating Alan went to the bookstall and bought the local evening paper in which we saw the headline, STONE; SCOTS AWAIT ARRIVAL. Then we read how a party of Scottish Nationalists was waiting on the border to convoy the Stone across. We laughed at the fantasy, but we were delighted at the press we were getting.

When we had finished eating, I again telephoned Bill, but he had gone out. Our worry for Kay was now very great. It was thirty six hours since she had trundled off with her part of the Stone, and she had not been heard of since. Not all houses had telephones, and she might be all right. On the other hand, if she were playing cat and mouse with the police in the Anglia, we ought to know about it, and perhaps create a diversion. The press were the obvious people to help, so I telephoned the news room of the *Bulletin*. After all, they had started us on our journey by printing that photograph of Wendy Wood twenty years before.

They owed me some information.

'Any news about the Stone?' I asked.

'Nothing new,' replied the reporter.

'Any arrests?' I asked.

'No none,' he said.

'Thank God for that,' I said, and then heard a flicker of interest in his voice.

'Who's speaking?'

'It's one of the crew who took it,' I told him. 'I'm 'phoning from Newcastle station.'

The man was excited, and questioned me about the whereabouts of the Stone. 'You don't expect me to answer that?' I asked indignantly, but I told him that it was safe in Scotland, having left Newcastle six hours earlier. Then I rang off.

From my knowledge of the press, I thought that they might print the story, but it was unlikely that they would tell the police beforehand. If they had something, they would not want to share it with anyone, and we would be across the Border before the police could concentrate all their people on the east side, perhaps giving Kay the chance to slip through on the west. The *Bulletin* did print the story. They said that I spoke without trace of an accent. Since I speak broad Paisley, and there is only one broader in all Scotland, and that's Barrhead, I can guess where yon reporter comes from.

We put as much distance between us and Newcastle station as we could, for we felt certain that the police would take some action on our call, even if it was later rather than sooner. Whatever action they took, if any, was not apparent to us. Perhaps they were beginning to see the futility of getting anything other than abuse and laughter from any Scots they stopped. North of Morpeth we did not see a single police patrol, and Berwick, the Border town, seemed empty of police as we drove through.

We crossed the Border about ten o'clock with a marvellous feeling of relief. The very trees and hedges seemed more friendly, and we knew that if we were ever hard pressed we would only have to knock on a door and a friend would open it. All Scotland was our fireside, and every Scotsman was our kin. Idly I thought of the last verses of Edinbane, and wondered if I would ever travel to Scotland and meet with closed doors and sour faces. I quoted to myself:

> Though I know that time must sever
> Every friendship, every tie.
> Yet I'm sure the years will never
> Change my welcoming in Skye.
>
> Must a day come long hereafter
> When I'll travel sure in vain,
> When I'll hear no lilt of laughter
> From the Inn at Edinbane?

That night the whole of Scotland was Edinbane.

Forty years on

The charming verses on 'Edinbane' are not great poetry, but they have a haunting quality, and date from the time in the late twenties or early thirties when John MacCormick stood as Scottish Nationalist candidate in Inverness-shire. He was their author. I still recite them to myself while driving about Scotland bound for the Circuit Courts.

John was a man of many graces, and when he died some of his friends, myself among them, thought of publishing his poetry as a memorial to him. It never came to anything, partly because he needed no memorial, and partly because any friend of John MacCormick was inevitably broke. Like attracted like. I wonder where his manuscripts are.

118

Chapter Seventeen

This was Scotland, but it was not home. Fifty seven miles lay between us and Edinburgh; Glasgow was forty seven miles beyond that. Our feeling of security that we were back across the Border was a false one, but it was comforting nonetheless. Scotland has its own system of law, and its criminal law is quite different from England's. I assured Alan that now we were in Scotland we would have the whole resources of Scottish Law to assist us against England. Alan doubted my knowledge of the law. I had doubts about it myself. Still, if anyone ever thinks that we are not two separate countries, let him have a pint in Coldstream, and then walk across the bridge over the Tweed, and have another in Cornhill. It's not just the beer that's different.

The excitement of being back from a different country quickly died. It is a beautiful road from Berwick to Edinburgh, but it was black dark and icy so we could not appreciate it. Shortly after midnight we arrived in Edinburgh. A thin freezing rain was falling and the streets gleamed wickedly. We were tired again, almost beyond speech. Our words fell slowly from slack lips, and we stared for many seconds before our senses perceived anything, yet we felt some quickening of the spirit as we came to Princes Street. The gardens were dark on our left, but high above them hung quivering, mysterious and unbodied the great bulk of the Castle. Down the High Street, crowded gable upon gable, were the ancient houses of the capital of Scotland. It was an empty capital waiting for the clash and clamour of the glory of life to be breathed back into it, but it was our capital nonetheless.

Up there on the hill the Scottish Estates had met and passed legislation far in advance of its time. The General Assemblies had convened and dethroned a Queen, and made a King, and driven out an invader. John Knox had walked these very streets shouting for reform. 'There shall be a school in every parish, and everyone

119

shall have the right to a university education,' he had thundered. It took fifty years for that dream to come true, but it was three centuries ahead of any other country nonetheless. Up there Montrose had gone quietly to his death in the shadow of buildings which still stood. The Covenant of 1638 had been signed in the Greyfriars Churchyard on the other side of the hill, and the Covenant of 1949 had been launched in the Assembly Hall which I could see as I drove along Princes Street. As I looked up at that close mass of Scottish history, I hoped that we too might have played our part, however small.

We wondered what our fellow countrymen were thinking about, and paused to buy the papers to see. We sat under a lamppost reading the early morning street editions of the papers. We were still full front page headline, and would remain there for weeks. The reports were not hostile, and we were delighted with them. English officialdom had risen to the bait, and was very indignant. There was much talk of sacrilege. Did they still hang people for sacrilege? It was obvious that there was a great deal of ruffled ermine at Westminster. That would be a favour to them. Complacency is bad for the arteries. The Dean's Christmas had been ruined. That was a pity, but it would teach him to be more careful when he meddled with stolen goods. We put away the papers and drove on. Things were simmering nicely.

Alan drove out of Edinburgh, and as we went through Corstorphine I again felt on the verge of collapse.

'Look out! Swerve! Swerve!' I suddenly shouted at him. I had a vivid hallucination that an old woman was hiding behind a lamp post waiting to throw herself under the car. The fright wakened us a little. Occasionally I sank into a dream and came near to the long foreshore of sleep, where nothing matters; occasionally we would talk, but each word had to be formed separately. Driving was an automatic chain of reactions, which sometimes went wrong, but never badly wrong. We were aiming for Alan's home on the outskirts of Barrhead.

We telephoned there from Harthill, and to our intense delight

Kay had been there only a few hours previously, before leaving to go to her home in Wester Ross. Overjoyed we tumbled back into the car. We were the last to make it, and despite fog, frost and ice, Alan made good time to Glasgow.

The city was like a pleasant dream. We knew it was true, but felt its unreality. I was preparing to say goodbye to Alan for I had expected to go up to my melancholy little room near Charing Cross. The bed would be unmade, there would be no fire, and the remains of my last meal would still be on the table. I was not looking forward to it. I lived like a pig, even if I preferred to grunt in comfort. I was grateful when Alan insisted that I should go out to Barrhead to spend the night at his home. We paused only to collect all the morning papers from the newsboy at the corner of Hope Street and Argyll Street. We could not read enough about ourselves.

Alan went forward to ring the bell with a great deal of fear. Here was no prodigal returned, but a criminal for whom Scotland Yard were consulting telepathists. He had wasted not his substance but his career. And no Scots father thinks lightly of his son's career. At any moment the police might descend on the house. In at least one view of the situation he had turned a happy home into a den of thieves, where each knock on the door might be the police. Alan rang the doorbell, while I waited in the shadows ready to run away. We need not have worried. When the door opened, and the welcome of the home had fallen across the threshold towards us, we were sucked into the security of the family, and the warmth of their happiness was wrapped like a blanket around us.

For a moment Mr Stuart was too overcome with pride and delight to speak. Then he seized us each by an arm and ushered us into a bright room with a leaping fire. I was introduced to Mrs Stuart, and to Alan's sister; a drink of whisky was put in our hands, and, in the babble of conversation we sat down and looked at the fire, and tried to believe that this was as real as the dark and the cold and the fog and the ice bound roads and the crucifixion of sleeplessness.

Our story ran through all the dream. We had never told it in all its fantastic detail. Now we tripped over each other to prompt our memories, and always we would be interrupted, and a newspaper would be thrust into our hands so that we might read what the world was saying. The fire leaped and crackled and blazed; the room was light; the people were our people; they spoke our language and knew us, and we knew them. They were our people. We could hardly believe it.

Before we went to bed we heard Kay's story, which was no less fascinating than ours. Alan's sister told it, for she had been the only one at home in the early evening when Kay had called.

When she left me, Kay realised that I had misdirected her and that she was not at Victoria, as I had said she was. She drove around asking her way, and finally struck Knightsbridge. It was at the traffic lights in Knightsbridge that she heard the great crash, and found her piece of the Stone lying in the road behind her. To this day I can imagine her grimace of exasperation at my carelessness in not shutting the boot properly. Kay is a small girl, yet she picked up that lump of sandstone, which weighed more than she did, and put it back into the car. This time she made sure that all was properly secured.

She drove on, certain that every noise she heard was the boot opening. Several times she stopped the car to make sure she had not lost her piece of the Stone on the road. Meanwhile she was asking her way all the time, trying to reach her Scots friend near Oxford, not Birmingham, as I had thought. She was certain that she would find asylum there.

At length she became worried. She had left a complete chain of people behind her who had directed a girl in a Ford Anglia to Oxford, and she was certain that they would rush to the police when her description was circulated. She saw a signpost for Birmingham, a place where she also had a friend. All this time she had been giving lifts to anyone who thumbed her. First she stopped for two old ladies, with whom she exchanged recipes, and then for a soldier who showed her a shortcut which saved her many miles. As well as being a Christian act, giving lifts was good camouflage, and may have saved her from the police.

When she neared Birmingham, she saw a great deal of police activity. At one place she saw police patrols checking every car that passed through their check point. She casually turned down a side road, drove back the way she had come, and probed out another route where there was less inspection.

At length she reached her friend's house. She stopped the car outside and rang the doorbell. Her friend opened the door, but before she could find a word to express her pleasure, Kay told her, 'I'm a fugitive. I've got part of the Stone of Destiny with me.'

Her friend was startled, as who would not be?

'It doesn't matter,' she said. 'You're a friend of mine and that's all that matters.'

Together they concocted a story to tell the girl's mother. They decided to say that Kay had been to Oxford to collect her brother's car, who was in the forces, and about to be posted to Korea. Since the roads were so bad she had decided to leave the car and go on by train. Kay's friend was English through and through. Now do you see why I prefer an honourable English person to an Anglicised Scot?

Kay was introduced to the mother, who thought her a very brave girl to have motored all the way from Oxford over such bad roads. For the rest of Christmas Day she sat playing party games, and trying to look as though she had had at least one night's sleep in the last three or four. When the announcement of our success came over the radio, it was the first that she had heard of it, for of course she had left me as I raced back to the Abbey. It was all that she could do to refrain from shouting with joy. Yet no one except her friend knew her secret, as she sat and played games and wore a paper hat.

Kay left the next day without the mother suspecting her guilt. I do not know if she ever found out. Certainly when I went to Birmingham a fortnight later to collect the piece of Stone and drive it home in the Anglia, she had no suspicions. Indeed I drove the lady into the centre of the town that day, and as we drove we wondered together where 'those nationalists' might have hidden the Stone. She did not know that part of it was only a yard behind her, and I did not tell her. I hope she has forgiven us for our deception.

Kay's story should be remembered wherever Scotswomen wish to honour their kind. Alan and I had each other to lean on, and we leaned heavily. I should not have liked to have made all the decisions myself, and to have come through them all unaccompanied. Kay did it. Alone she made all the right decisions, calmly making her way through police cordons in a car that was sought by the police, for there were photographs of Ford Anglias in all the newspapers, and people everywhere were on the look out for them. To do something in company is one thing. But to do it alone, making your own decisions, and making the right ones is a totally different matter. No wonder I have always thought her quite beyond praise. I saw little of her after that Christmas. She went off a few weeks later to teach at Duncraig Castle School in Wester Ross, and in all the years since these few days together we have scarcely met. It has been one of the great regrets of my life that I never really got to know her. I have never known whether to go and see her would be a trespass and intrusion, or a welcome reunion. Her account of our adventure together would make interesting reading. Perhaps her brave kindness is the cause of her silence. She could tell a tale of my bungling, and of my selfish arrogance, but she hasn't. She, more than anyone else, was the powerhouse of our success, yet I have had fame from it which I do not want. We could have done nothing without her.

Early that morning in Alan's house we drank a toast to her, and emptied our glasses. A meal was waiting for us, but we were too tired to eat. Common decency howled for a bath, but common decency went unheard. We looked on our beds with eyes that crawled. Stiff thighed and weary we fell into them. There were hot water bottles in them, but we had time only to feel their warmth before we fell into a deep sleep.

Forty years on
I have been tired often since, but never as tired as I was that morning.
Yet youth can cope. When, in my sixties, I sailed to the Azores in a
twenty-seven foot boat with my son, I grew so exhausted that it was only
my son who pulled me through. But that was exhaustion, not mere
tiredness. I think I was right in my assessment expressed here and there
in these pages on the subject of lack of sleep. It does stop you being
frightened, and you always have a little more than you think you have, to
pull out when the occasion arises.

Chapter Eighteen

Before we had gone to bed I had asked, as firmly and politely as I dared, to be called at eight o'clock. Sleep is a good thing, but it can be taken in too large dozes. We were safely home, but much remained to be done. We had only started. Even as we fell unconscious into bed we were thinking of what the next step should be. We had the car to clean of all evidence, and our compatriots to see; we had to meet Councillor Gray and John MacCormick to make our report; we had to meet Bill Craig, and give him a fuller account of the Stone's hiding place to make certain that he could find it in the event of our arrest. Above all, we had to get into our usual haunts and act in a normal fashion, for our absence might have been noticed. I was on particularly dangerous ground here, for I was seldom far distant from the University. My prolonged absence would already have done no good.

When we were called I awakened immediately and lay happily for a moment thinking of success. I was going out to face my Glasgow accomplices, to report to them how we had succeeded beyond any reasonable expectations. That would be a pleasant thing to do. I was going to rejoin the society of my other friends, to appear normal to them while we discussed the Stone, with my special knowledge seething and bubbling under my equanimity.

I had a hot bath and a hot breakfast. My stiffness had disappeared and my tiredness had been wiped away. I was on my toes physically as well as mentally. The curtain had rung down on Act I. I was changing myself from the tired chauffeur into the social buffoon, who would be an object of contempt rather than suspicion. We would try to out-scarlet the Scarlet Pimpernel. We would talk about the Stone until we became Stone bores. In our cups we would boast that we had taken it, or else that we had had a plan ready to take it if someone had not forestalled us. We would swear that we had guns and bombs and gelignite ready prepared, and hint darkly what we would be doing with it, if only something was not preventing us. We would talk like any other young extremists of the Nationalist movement. It was the safest thing we could do. We knew that the Glasgow police were far too intelligent ever to bother about any of the avowed extremists. And although Scotland Yard would probably be taken in, they were too far away to hear any such talk.

I left my torn coat with Mrs Stuart, and was given an old one of Alan's. I was also given an old wrist watch to replace the one I had lost in the Abbey. The watch did not go, and every quarter of an hour I had to seek some privacy to advance the hands. The watch, which had broken from my wrist when I wrestled with the Stone in the Abbey, was the principal clue the police then had. Its photograph featured again and again in the newspapers. In those days not to wear a watch on your wrist meant that you were a very suspicious character indeed. Or so we all thought.

Fully prepared to meet the world, Alan and I went out to start the car. It took us over an hour to get it going, and we had to run it a hundred yards downhill before it fired. Yet this was the car which in the hour of need outside the Abbey had fired instantly, and allowed me to get the Stone away. Once back in Glasgow it knew it was near its stable. It developed some form of pulmonary disease in the carburettor, and seemed constantly on the verge of death. In its twelve or thirteen years of life I am certain that it had never been driven so far for so long as it had been driven by us. Yet not until our greatest need was past did it start to complain. Some cars have souls.

I went straight up to the University Union. It was of course the Christmas vacation, and the place should have been deserted. To my surprise all the familiar figures were about, and as I went forward to the fireplace, which, as James Bridie said, is the hub of the University, one of my friends detached himself from a group of students and came forward to congratulate me.

'Don't congratulate me,' I said, highly flattered nevertheless. 'You're being far too complimentary.' Solemnly we discussed who

127

might have done the deed. This man was accounted for; that man might have done it, but he drank too much to keep a secret; another had been talking about doing it for years, but he was a vainglorious lout with no ability; still another claimed that he had been there, but could make no statement at present.

'Well, I'm beaten,' I said. 'I reckoned I knew every Nationalist in Scotland, and I still can't put my finger on who did it.' Then I mused for a moment. 'Oh! I would have given my right hand to be there,' I burst out. I glanced at my watch, still pointing to the last hour I had set it at. 'Well time flies,' I said, and passed on.

The experience was one we all had, time and time again. All things considered, there was remarkably little suspicion. There was bound to be some leakage, for some of the people I had approached, who had refused to go to London with us, were thus in the secret. Likewise Gavin and Alan had been forced to confide in a few of their friends to safeguard their alibis. Some of these people tried to guard us from ourselves, and told us that we were too interested in the Stone. Yet every Nationalist was interested, and the proof of our double bluff was the extent to which it worked. We were discovered in the end by patient police enquiry, and it is one of the most remarkable things about the whole enterprise that not one word came from those who knew us, to give the police any hint. They had to work from the outside without the help of any informer or tip-off agent. Indeed, three months later, when I was roped in for questioning, I was delighted to be told what one of my fellows had said of me:

'What! Ian Hamilton have anything to do with the Stone! The only person who would suspect Ian Hamilton is Ian Hamilton.'

I've smiled with grim pleasure at that remark ever since.

When I left the group at the Union fireplace I went in search of Bill Craig. While I was wandering round in an indeterminate fashion looking for him I suddenly saw Gavin. He was in the centre of a press of students, loudly averring that I was the man who had stolen the Stone of Destiny, of that he was certain. There was no doubt about it. I asked him where he had been himself over Christmas, and he said that he had been following me all the way to Westminster. In the ensuing uproar of conversation, I was able to prise him apart from his friends, and we found an unused committee room, and fell into conversation.

I had not seen him since that amazing hour when Alan and I had left him forlorn and alone somewhere near the Old Kent Road. That he had already arrived home we had learned from Bill Craig, but I was interested to know what series of circumstances had kept him from meeting us at Reading. First, however, he had to know what had happened to us. I told him briefly, for I was already getting tired of repeating the story, and I wanted to hear his.

When we had left him he had walked aimlessly for what seemed an endless while, until life had come back into the city. Then he had gone for something to eat, and in a restaurant had noticed a man regarding him with suspicion. He finished his meal and left, but try as he would to dislodge his pursuer, he was certain he was still being followed. He had walked round the town, still trailed by the policeman, and since he had not wanted to lead his shadow to our rendezvous at Reading, he had taken the train to Rugby. At Rugby he felt that he had shaken off the man, but since he could not get a train from Rugby to Reading in time to meet us that day, he had gone on to Crewe. From Crewe he came straight back to Glasgow.

I was relieved to hear Gavin's story, and after he had assured me that he was not at present under observation by the police we parted. I had every sympathy with Gavin. Keeping pressing on, as Alan and I had had to do, stopped us from ever looking over our shoulders, but, if we had not had the company of each other to feed our courage, I have little doubt we would have acted as Gavin had acted. I left him and continued my search for Bill Craig.

I found him on that Mount Olympus of the University, the Union Board Members' dining room. I knocked on the door and looked in. This was the Establishment, and I have ever been excluded from establishments. One of the men who had been unable to come to London with us looked at me with a half-knowing, half-amazed smile. Bill saw me and made some excuse to leave his meal and come outside to meet me. The rest of the Union Board went on eating.

As soon as he had closed the door behind him, Bill clasped me by the hand and marched me along the corridor, patting me warmly on the back. He was as excited as a child and I was no more calm. We locked ourselves in a committee room (he had a set of keys) and talked mightily. We had much to tell each other. I gave him the main outline of the story, and he gasped with amazement at all the right places. Already it had sunk into my consciousness as fact, and the wonder of it had been accepted. It was in the past, and I was looking into the future, which is the only place worth looking at.

When I told him that we had broken it, he looked thoughtful for a moment, and then said, 'Place not your faith in Archbishops. He should have guarded it better.'

I chuckled at his logic, and then listened to him as he told me that Scotland was alive with interest, and I could well believe it, for I had seen it for myself. I left Bill, agreeing to meet him later in Craig's Coffee-room in Sauchiehall Street, where he had arranged for me to have an afternoon coffee with John MacCormick and Bertie Gray.

I left the Union to walk down town. I was too excited to stay in one place, yet I had nowhere to go. As I walked down Gibson Street I met Tom Dawson of the *Daily Mail*. Tom had come up to the University a year earlier than I had, and we had lived together in the same University hostel. I knew him well. He was slim and nervous, constantly active, and always thrusting forward. He was already making a name for himself in journalism, because he would never rest while he had a story on his mind. I was not pleased to meet him. I knew he had me on his mind.

'Hullo,' he said.

I said, 'Hullo.'

'Are you in a hurry?' he asked.

''Not specially,' I said.

'Come and have a drink then.'

I fidgeted, but I felt that the best thing was to go with him. I like Tom, and if I were to rush away, I could only arouse his suspicion.

He ordered two half pints, because he had an expense account. I eyed mine sourly. 'I expect you'll be claiming for double whiskies on this,' I said.

He smiled wryly. 'I don't want to buy you whisky in case you think I'm trying to get you to talk.' He laughed, and looked at me shrewdly through his laughter.

'You're another!' I cried in simulated delight. 'All morning people have been accusing me of stealing the Stone of Destiny. It's the highest compliment I've ever been paid.'

He looked almost pained. 'Where were you over the week-end, Ian?' he asked.

'I was at home,' I said, wishing fervently that I had been able to establish an alibi. Had I attempted to, by telling them my intentions, my parents would have done all they could to stop me.

'Ian, Ian', said Tom shaking his head. 'I 'phoned your home as soon as the news broke. Your mother hasn't seen you for weeks.'

I cast about for a feeble excuse and gave it. He did not believe it. I did not expect him to. I had known that my guilt was obvious. It had been obvious to Tom Dawson from the beginning, and it was no doubt equally obvious to the police. I felt a happy recklessness, that was tarnished only by a bitter anger at Tom. I would have preferred not to have been sold by a friend. Surely he could have kept his suspicions to himself.

'What am I to do? he asked.

I looked at him. 'That's up to you,' I said at last.

'You'd better get a decent alibi before the police come,' he said.

I drank my beer. 'What do you mean?' I asked. The barman approached our end of the bar. We moved over to a quiet corner.

'Ian,' he said. 'I may be a newspaperman and I may have the greatest story ever. I'm hoping to go to Fleet Street soon, and I'm not much interested in Home Rule. But by God, I'm a Scotsman first. Don't worry. I'll never sell you.'

It is times like these that make me very humble. What else can a man say?

We shook hands on it and I went down town. Thereafter, while the newspaper world went mad, and bid and rebid for news of the Stone, Tom went quietly about his work and said nothing. He could have retired on the price of that story, but he kept his word. He kept his honour also, and that perhaps is the greatest thing of all. In the whole of this strange story it is the people who played the lesser parts who come out of it without blemish.

Tom Dawson was the first, but I don't believe he was the only one. When the trail became hot other journalists must have stumbled on information which might have been valuable to the police, slept on it, and by the morning had conveniently forgotten it. To a very real extent the love of community had become identified with the Stone of Destiny, and patriotism was proved to be a stronger motive than professional success and love of money. What was true of journalists was true also of people as a whole. As the Stone was passed from hand to hand many people became involved in the secret. Not one of them spoke or availed themselves of the rich rewards which were offered for information. It was like the '45 over again.

That there were would-be informers, I know. I even know who some of them were. I bear no animosity towards them. Their political views troubled their conscience, but in the end they had nothing to tell. The startling fact remains that after two centuries of quiet history a country reawakened, covered the people who had acted in their name, and would not give them up.

Forty years on

Tom Dawson went to Fleet Street and I lost touch with him. Then many years later I met him quite by chance on a train. He had found a niche for himself in his chosen profession, and had never regretted the decision he had made. Only a journalist, or one who has had much to do with journalists, can understand the measure of his self sacrifice, and I write about him with pride. I ruefully claim some reflected credit. This story shows me up as a ruthless, self centred prig. Yet I cannot have been all that bad if I held the friendship of a man like Tom Dawson.

Chapter Nineteen

As arranged by Bill, I went to Craig's Coffee-room in Sauchiehall Street at four o'clock. I was to meet John MacCormick and Bertie Gray. I was becoming quite familiar with their Christian names by now. Bill arrived first, and when I joined him, we sat and sipped our coffee among all the businessmen whom we felt were pointing us out to one another. Since I had been approached by Tom Dawson I was certain that people were already looking at me as the criminal. All around us we could hear the hum of conversation, and the word Stone was often audible. By God, if we could get Glasgow businessmen to talk of something other than money and golf, we had worked a miracle! Among them I felt like Cain at a police conference. The feeling passed off quite quickly, but we had only been home for a few hours, and were not yet accustomed to what we felt as exposure. By the next day I was able to play the innocent fool with a great deal of ease. Indeed, when the police questioned me towards the end of the whole episode, I had so convinced myself of my innocence that I was highly indignant when I was aroused from my bed at seven in the morning. This afternoon, however, I was nervous, and when we had gulped our scalding coffee, Bill and I fled down to the basement and hid in the lavatory.

We had been in the lavatory only two minutes when a lawyer's clerk came in. I am reasonably certain he was a lawyer's clerk, but to us he looked like a detective. We stopped washing our hands (we had washed them twice already) and I nonchalantly made for the door. Bill waited behind to see if I was followed.

In the hallway I met Councillor Gray coming in to keep his coffee engagement. He saw me. I saw him. We walked towards one another, then, remembering who I was, I walked straight past him and out of the door. Had I not been to London? Were not the police even now trailing me? Should I not show him what a dangerous man I was — too dangerous to recognise a friend? It was fine fun. Bertie enjoyed it too.

Outside in Bertie's car I met John MacCormick. He looked as small and drawn and tired as ever. What we had done was only a fraction of what he had done for Scotland. As I climbed in beside him, he smiled at me. 'Congratulations,' he said. 'You pulled it off.' It was praise indeed. Every mile had been worth it.

Councillor Gray returned, followed by Bill. The lawyer's clerk had washed his hands and gone, fresh and hygenic, to drink his coffee. Sheepishly I explained to the Councillor why I had ignored him, and we drove off.

Riding round the town I told them my story. We did not have much time so I made it as brief as possible. I could talk freely in the car, for there could be no eavesdroppers. In the days to come we were to hold many such councils in Bertie's car, for John did not have one. There is more money in tomb-stones than in law. When my recital came to the bit about hiding the Stone I was questioned closely. 'Was I sure I could find it again? Was it safely hidden? Was there any chance of someone stumbling on it?' To all of these questions I was able to give satisfactory answers.

Then it was my turn to ask questions. Both the older men were delighted at the public reaction. Only the previous night the Dean of Westminster had been on the radio lamenting 'this cunningly planned and carefully executed crime.' If you get away with a crime it's always cunningly planned and carefully executed. Once you're caught, everyone tells you how clumsy you were. The Dean's comment on our action was high praise. The authorities were determined to treat the affair as one of the first magnitude, and that suited us admirably. If they had ignored us we would have felt fools. On the other hand the Dean had said that the King was sorely troubled about the loss of the Stone. Something should be done about that. We arranged that we should meet that night and petition His Majesty, reaffirming our loyalty to him, and setting out our reasons for taking the Stone. Bertie had served in the trenches in the first world war, and was entitled to be called Major Gray if he wanted, which he didn't. Bill and I had served towards the end of the second war. The King did not have a monopoly of loyalty, but he represented a lot that was valuable to the two countries. We wanted then, as I have wanted ever since, a dual monarchy, not a republic, so it was time to make some public statement about our aims.

Before that we had another engagement. A newsreel crew was keen to make a film of the reactions of the people in the streets of Glasgow to the removal of the Stone from London. Councillor Gray had been invited to attend as a man in the street, and he was anxious that I should accompany him. I was not loth. The opportunity for the criminal to watch the filming of the reactions to his crime is one not lightly to be missed. There was no reason why I should not be present. I was a minor official in the Covenant Association, the assistant editor of its journal, *The New Covenanter*, and in that capacity my interest in the proceedings was obvious. Indeed, that night, in my own journalistic capacity, I did some pretty dead-pan interviewing of the people present. Irony is a Scottish vice. We overindulge in it with as much joy as we overindulge in drink, and we enjoy it even more. The filming was something of an anti-climax. In order to strike a balance, the producer sought people to condemn the outrage. In the crowded studio he could find none. I thought for a moment of taking up the minority view, ever a position in which I'm at home, but I was still nervous of unnecessary risks. I am now sorry I missed that opportunity. It is the temptations you don't succumb to that you regret later on. In the end Bertie roundly condemned us all, but anonymously so that his face did not appear on screen. A day or two later we watched the result in the cinema with great amusement.

It was the first of many such interviews. Television was then in its infancy. Only London had it, but there were the foreign crews as well. They came from all over the world, and as I was now acting as a sort of private secretary to John MacCormick I attended many of these filmings. They afforded me much quiet amusement. They also made me despair. It was such a foreign way of life to me and it still is. To spectate rather than to do, is a sort of death.

Who wants to watch other peoples' lives, when their own is there to be lived? Yet to stand behind the camera, hearing events solemnly discussed, and knowing that I was the author of these events, gave me a feeling of insufferable superiority which I suffered very easily. It was outrageously smug, but it was also very satisfying. I should have been garrotted with one of the many leads and cables which snaked across John's drawing room, and probably would have been, had the crews had any suspicion. They never had. Not one of these television personalities ever took me aside to ask precisely what I was doing there. It is the only television role I want to play.

It was probably the best camouflage we could adopt. As happy, talkative, frank supporters of our Lord Rector we were living one life, and our double bluff threw much suspicion from us. As people not averse to taking risks, we lived another life no less real than the first. We were careful to leave no pathway from one identity to the other. People are a strange creation, and on meeting each other we touch only at the furthest frontiers of our being. One person knows hardly anything about another. We guarded our frontiers and no one knew that there was a totally different person behind the one that was on show. It was a happy time, far happier than when the dreadful spotlight of fame shone on us a few months later. That was miserable beyond belief. But for the moment we could enjoy playing out the ploy in anonymity.

The next part of the ploy was decided in John MacCormick's flat at midnight of that first night we were back home. Bill, John, Bertie, and myself, met to decide what to do next. We decided that we had to issue some sort of press statement, although, in my view, the action spoke far louder than any words. The press, with the melancholy exception of the *Glasgow Herald*, had been favourable. *The Glasgow Herald* was then edited by Attila the Hun; the woman's page by Attila the Hen. The prevailing opinion among us was that something should be said. As yet no one knew whether the Stone had been taken by Anarchists, Communists, or honest souvenir hunters. In addition, His Majesty was distressed. It was our plain duty to reaffirm our loyalty and make it clear that we meant no treason nor disrespect. That was my elders' view and I went along with it. At the same time we wished to let the King know that we had no respect for his advisers, who were misruling Scotland, and against whom all our actions were directed.

After much discussion we drew up the following petition.

The Petition of certain of His Majesty's most loyal and obedient subjects to His Majesty King George the Sixth humbly sheweth:

That His Majesty's Petitioners are the persons who removed the Stone of Destiny from Westminster Abbey:

That in removing the Stone of Destiny they have no desire to injure His Majesty's property nor to pay disrespect to the Church of which he is temporal head:

That the Stone of Destiny is, however, the most ancient symbol of Scottish nationality and, having been removed from Scotland by force and retained in England in breach of the pledge of His Majesty's predecessor, King Edward III of England, its proper place of retention is among His Majesty's Scottish people, who, above all, hold this symbol dear:

That therefore His Majesty's petitioners will most readily return the Stone to the safe keeping of His Majesty's officers if His Majesty will but graciously assure them that in all time coming the Stone will remain In Scotland in such of His Majesty's properties or otherwise as shall be deemed fitting by him:

That such an assurance will in no way preclude the use of the Stone in any coronation of any of his Majesty's successors whether in England or in Scotland:

That His Majesty's humble petitioners are prepared to submit to His Majesty's Minister or representatives proof that they are the people able, willing and eager to restore the Stone of Destiny to the keeping of His Majesty's officers:

That His Majesty's petitioners who have served him in peril and in peace, pledge again their loyalty to him, saving always their right and duty to protest against the actions of his Ministers if such actions are contrary to the wishes or the spirit of His Majesty's Scottish people.

In witness of the good faith of His Majesty's petitioners the following information concerning a watch left in Westminster Abbey on December 25th 1950 is appended—(1) the main spring of the watch was recently repaired; (2) the bar holding the right-hand wrist strap to the watch had recently been broken and soldered.

This information is given in lieu of signature by His Majesty's petitioners being in fear of apprehension.

Forty years on

And so we started to play games. I suppose there was really nothing else we could do, but the wording of that petition still makes me grue. It is impossible nowadays to convey the idolatry with which the Royal family were then regarded. Our present Queen never had a baby. She aye gave birth to a prince or a princess. Look at the Court circulars for the times and you will see what I mean. Thus when the King let his concern be known publicly, we had to go warily. His concern was only for what he regarded as the loss of Royal property. He wanted his thing back. Privately we learned that he had a superstitous fear that the loss portended the end of his dynasty. All this was so much nonsense, but we had to watch public opinion.

Dynasty or not, even the Scots were divided. There was jubilation at the return of the Stone, and vexation that the King was vexed, so I suppose that we had to do something to keep public opinion with us. Behind the formal, indeed grandiloquent wording of the Petition there lay a perfectly reasonable statement of our position. Keep the Stone in

139

Scotland, and we will hand it back. We had to make our position public, and a letter to the King seemed the best way.

Best way or not, it nearly chokes me forty years on to quote the Petition. Indeed I have cut out much of the humbug contained in the 1952 edition of this book. It was needed then, but we have grown beyond that need. Royalty is all right, but has no part in constitutional affairs. We don't have hereditary professors of Constitutional Law, and hereditary heads of Constitutions are a similar absurdity. A hereditary Head of a Church is a lovely piece of English dottiness, but no one really thinks that the sovereign is divine any longer, or do they? I am so often taken for a republican because I never attend the Queen's garden party, or any other of the Royal functions to which from time to time I'm invited, that I wonder. I'm not a republican. No arid view keeps me from Holyrood. I am far too much of a traditionalist for that. The truth is I can't be bothered. Monarchy is all right, and I'm a monarchist, because people love the monarchy. You can't abolish something people love to cheer. Nonsense it may be, but it is a loveable nonsense. Besides, who else could we have petitioned in these circumstances?

The petition caused the pot to boil over once again. Indeed had the palace had anything so vulgar as a chip pan, it would have caused a palace chip-pan fire. The press loved it. The Glasgow Herald *had a first leader on it, in which they managed to say that it was the product of a mature legal brain, and the effusion of mealy mouthed romantics. I've never quite forgiven the* Glasgow Herald *for that last remark. It was too near the truth.*

And yet, and yet, I wonder if I am truly reporting what I felt for the monarchy then, and still feel for it, for all its faults. That old gentleman, King George VI, had led us, Scotland as well as England, through one of the most dangerous times in our history. I mean that he personally symbolised us all, not Churchill, who was a political figure, not universally loved. It was the King who was one with the nation. By a curious inversion it is the sovereign who leads the common people, and sometimes speaks for us also. I can still recite verbatim the closing quotation of his address to the nation, broadcast live on Christmas Day 1940, when we were alone and the days were indeed dark. Imagine it spoken in that

140

curious hesitant monotone voice he had been forced bravely to adopt to overcome his nervous stammer so that he could speak live to his people. This is how he ended his speech:

> *'I said to the man who stood at the gate of the year, Give me a light that I may tread out into the unknown, and the man said to me, Go out into the darkness and put your hand into the hand of God, for it is better than a light, and safer than a known way.'*

Oh yes, we were right to reaffirm our loyalty. Anyone who could find words such as these deserved all we could give.

Chapter Twenty

Having prepared the Petition, the next problem was how to convey it to the King. A tuppenny stamp and a post box was the obvious solution. After all, it was His Royal Mail. But that would not serve our purpose. While petitioning the King, we were also persuading the people, and whatever method we used had to be one which permitted the people to read the correspondence. This was no time for secret diplomacy. From now on everyone was in the game, and whatever we did was open to criticism. Give the public the chance to cheer your actions, and you also give them the right to boo. This communication demanded something more than a licked stamp and a sealed envelope. It had to be made public.

If the press could get access to it, so would the public. The traditional way is to nail the communication to some public door, as we did with a later communication by nailing it to the door of St. Giles Cathedral. The obvious door for our Petition was the door to the Abbey of Scone, from where the Stone had originally been stolen by Edward of England. Unfortunately, Scone Abbey has no door; indeed there is no longer an Abbey of Scone. We were some hundreds of years too late. It had all been knocked down to provide material for building Scone Palace, the home of the Earl of Mansfield. Things were getting difficult, and since the English press were referring to the Stone as the Stone of Scone, we decided to use the door to Scone Post Office as the next best thing. As this could only be done in the hours of darkness, I went off to get some sleep before setting out.

Bill wakened me two hours later. I copied out the petition in false handwriting, being careful to handle the paper only with gloves, for I wished to leave no fingerprints. The false handwriting was not a wise idea. Scotland Yard's department of holography is probably more skilful than its department of telepathy, and I was taking a needless risk. Still, we had no typewriter immediately available, and the petition was in a hurry. It was coming on for

4.00 a.m. when we finally went for the car, which had had to be kept in an overnight garage because of the intense cold.

We started it with difficulty and drove off north. As we drove, we argued. I took the view that the petition deserved a better fate than being pinned to the door of a country post office. Post offices are mundane things; village post offices are no exception. It was quite likely that it would be torn down and put in a dead letter box because it didn't have a stamp. I wanted to deliver it somewhere else.

Scone was still the ideal place, but not the post office. Then I remembered that the Earl of Mansfield had come out strongly in favour of our action. I can take Earls or leave them, but their very title makes people think that they are something special, and to have an Earl on our side, as well as all the rest of public opinion was too good to be ignored. I wanted to use the Earl, just as we were using the King. Such a scheme, of course, had its dangers. The nobleman might set a trap for us, and hand us over to the police. Yet I was not afraid of that. I believed that honour was far too real a thing among the aristocracy for him to betray me after he had given me a safe conduct.

In Perth, we stopped outside the post office, looked his name up in the directory and telephoned him. Although I would not give my name he came to the telephone almost immediately. I had the insolence to ask if his telephone was being tapped, although the insolence had common sense behind it. It gave him a chance to withdraw immediately, and also impressed him with the necessity for prudence. His caution would, I hoped, be a reflection of mine.

He assured me that to the best of his knowledge his telephone was quite innocent, and I asked him if I could come to visit him. He was rather reluctant, for he was engaged with his guests, but when I told him the nature of my business his tone immediately changed.

'I'm just leaving for the moors with my guests,' he told me, 'and I don't think it would be wise to cancel that. Could you come and see me at six o'clock?'

I assured him that that would suit admirably and rang off.

I drove Bill to Perth Station, for he was now leaving me to go back to Glasgow. I was sorry about that for I enjoyed his company, but as President of the Union he had to interview a new pastry cook.

I had ten hours to put in before I went out to Scone to visit the Earl, but the time would not be wasted. My parents were retired and lived at Ballinluig, less than thirty miles north of Perth, and it had been in my mind that I would visit them. Before I had set out for London I had left Bill a pathetic letter addressed to them. It was a note explaining why I was in the jail. He had been told to post it if things went wrong. We had burned the letter, but now I was to face them in the flesh.

As I drove over the familiar miles I became more and more nervous. I have a profound respect for my parents, but I have interpreted their teachings in many ways which they do not understand. I thought they might be vexed and angry, and consider only the lawlessness of my actions. Oh, I had all my arguments ready, but have you ever tried arguing with an elder of the Kirk?

These were my arguments. Up until the Union of 1707, Scots law was founded not on the supremacy of Parliament, but on the sovereignty of the people. If a law was oppressive, or against public policy, or even if it was obtuse and unworkable, it could be disobeyed and would fall into desuetude and be forgotten. In the last resort the real power in the Kingdom was not the Parliament which passed the law, but the law courts and the people who took it upon their conscience to ignore a law which they considered to be unworkable. I lived, however, in a time when the Anglo-Teutonic doctrine of the supremacy of the central government had usurped the Scottish doctrine of the supremacy of the people. My academic arguments may have been good Scots law, but they would not have been accepted at the Old Bailey. Nor, I grimly thought, would they cut any ice with my father.

As I passed through Guay and Kindallachan on the way to

144

meet him, I was afraid. I had lost my watch, and it had been a present from him. I had ruined my overcoat, which he had made. I had broken innumerable laws, and now I was trying to make him an accessory to my crimes. Above all, I had ruined my career, a career which he had make great financial sacrifices to further. When I reached Ballinluig, and skidded round the corner at the garage I felt like the criminal I was.

I drove up the lane at the side of the house. My mother was amazed and delighted to see me, for I had not been home since the summer. I greeted her uneasily and went into the house. She followed me in, taking off her apron as she came. I sat down on a chair and felt dreadfully ill at ease. The family surroundings inflamed my guilty conscience, and I could scarcely look anywhere with comfort.

My father had heard my voice, and he came into the room a moment later. His thin spare face was ruddy with health, and his eyes lit up as he came straight across to me and shook my hand. I answered his questions in monosyllables.

'Yes. I am well.'

'No. I'm not making a long stay.' I shrank from plunging into the explanation, and the conversation wandered off at a tangent. The weather had been bad, but everyone was well; my father's bees seemed to be surviving the winter, but the ground was too hard for digging.

'How did you come up?' he asked.

'By car,' I said. I saw the surprise in their faces. I had long since sold the expensive motor bike he had given me. It had gone to eke out my standard of not too quiet living. I could see that I could procrastinate no longer.

'What time is it?' I asked, looking at my bare wrist, for I had taken off the Stuarts' watch before I came in.

They looked at me queerly, for the clock on the mantelpiece stared me in the face.

'I've lost my watch,' I said, and added, 'in Westmister Abbey.'

My mother started and looked to see if I was joking. My lost watch was the most publicised clue to the whole episode. Its photograph was in all the newspapers. So everyone joked about losing their watch in Westminster Abbey. She saw I was not joking.

'Was it you?' she asked. 'Was it you who took the Stone? We thought you would have a hand in it.'

I turned to my father. A broad grin was spreading over his face. 'Well done,' he said. 'Well done. I haven't been so proud of anything for a long time.'

In face of the expected anger and tears, I had found instead the blessing of parental pride. Here was not anger but joy. The ways of one generation differ from another, yet he understood everything I had done. I had always respected my father, and now in turn I had won his respect. That was the hour of my greatest triumph.

I told them nothing of the story, and they asked for nothing. The story was responsibility, and I wanted to spare them that. All they wanted to know was if the Stone was in the Serpentine, which the police were then dredging. I assured them that it was not, and we laughed happily at the frolics of Scotland Yard.

The time I had to spend with them was very short, and yet my mother managed to feed me several meals in the interval, for she said I looked thin and white. I told her it was only lack of sleep. As I ate, my father asked me if he could help us in any way. I knew that he was keen to hide the Stone, as what Scot was not, but that was a risk I could not take. I did not want him to be the custodian of the Stone while his son was on trial for removing it. That was no job for a father.

There was, however, one job he could do for me. It might yet make the difference between success and failure, but I hesitated to ask him. He could lie to the police and give me an alibi. Sooner or later they would come to me and ask me how I had spent Christmas, and the simplest way to lull their suspicions was to say that I had been home.

'What will you do when the police come?' he asked.

'I don't know,' I said.

Now my father loved the truth. Quite apart from the rigorous and stern Calvinist religion which he practised, he loved the truth beyond anything I ever knew. I used to think that he loved it even more than his wife and family. I have tried to copy him over the years, with what success I know not, but truth was regarded by us all as a virtue in itself. It is one of the very few virtues which can stand without being propped up by any other. I forget which of us mentioned my need for an alibi, but he undertook to give me one for Christmas. It was the only Christmas present I've ever valued. Staunch old Presbyterians of my father's school find it easier to do anything for a cause than to lie for it, yet that was all that was in his power to do and he did it without hesitation, and without any indication of the sacrifice he was making. It was his sacrifice and his service. To this day I do not think he did it for his son. He did it for his country.

Together we went into the details. We fixed my time of arrival and departure, and agreed that I had hitch-hiked home. No bus conductor or railway porter could inadvertently contradict that. Anxiously my mother and father memorised the details so that our three versions of the story might tally.

I took my leave with my father's blessing. 'Don't worry,' he said. 'We'll stand by you whatever happens.'

They waved to me as I backed out onto the road and turned south into the heavy twilight to keep my appointment with the Earl of Mansfield. I was leaving one nobleman to meet another.

Forty years on

The statement of the law which I made to myself on my way to meet my father and mother, and wrote down shortly thereafter, is a peculiarly Scottish conception. It has no part in English law, which stems from the Norman Conquest. In England the theory is that every law must be obeyed, or society will fall asunder. We must all do as we're told. Germany had the same rule. It led to the Nuremberg War Crimes Tribunals.

John MacCormick and I later tested the theory, arguing that Parliament was at least bound by the Treaty of Union. In 1953 we raised an action against the Lord Advocate challenging the right of the Queen to call

147

herself Elizabeth the Second in Scotland. There never had been an Elizabeth the First of Scotland. Indeed the painted old harridan who held that title was a great enemy of Scotland, and only an English queen. We lost the action, as we knew we would, but we got from the Court an important opinion on the constitutional position of Scots law. I quote one line from the judgment of Lord President Cooper, 'The principle of the unlimited Sovereignty of Parliament is a distinctively English principle which has no counterpart in Scottish Constitutional Law.' That quotation is from the Opinion of the First Division of the Court of Session, delivered on 30 July 1953. The case of MacCormick and Another against the Lord Advocate is one of the leading cases in Scottish Constitutional Law.

In the present time the argument waxes strongly. It was used by me and others as one of the many arguments in support of our non-payment of the poll tax. The fact that the tax has been withdrawn is an example of how the people can force a Government to change its mind. Sometimes the people are ahead of the law.

Chapter Twenty-One

Snow was blocking the high passes to the North of Ballinluig, so I was almost the only car on the road. The local provision merchants still kept up their service to isolated farms, and I met an occasional local bus and the odd private car. It was not safe to meet oncoming traffic at any speed higher than a crawl, and overtaking was impossible. Frost crept in with the darkness and the road shone black and evil under an uneasy cloud-blocked sky. I began to realise that I was going to be late for my appointment.

The steering of the car was giving me great trouble. The Ballinluig garage had done what they could for it, by injecting massive amounts of grease into the steering joints, but they had told me the whole thing should be scrapped. Garages love giving bad news. I crept along, peering into the yellow beam of the headlights, forcing concentration on the snaky black roads. The hills, like two friends, convoyed me on either hand, but the blackness had that grey quality which accompanies damp frost, so I could not see them. Still I knew they were there, and they comforted me.

At Murthly, where the hills come down into a series of fat ripples, I turned from the main road and struck across country. I had carefully noted the position of the Earl's estate on the map, and I thought that I had memorised the route. I soon found that in the dark all the roads seemed the same, and I was as hopelessly lost as I had been in the Old Kent Road two days before. Roads which appeared to lead in one direction treacherously turned in another. Those I sought directions from were again the village idiots, or strangers there themselves. What strangers were doing in the wilds of Perthshire on that bleak night I did not know. It was all very sinister.

Yet, although I was late for my appointment, the delay did little harm. Earls can wait. The fear of meeting a man of his rank did not trouble me greatly. Scotland has never been a feudal country and lords are just commoners with titles. The country schools have produced peers as well as ploughmen and professors, and will do so again when England stops lowering our education system to a level with its own. Yet it was a new situation. I was passing from the level of action, where a man is accepted for what he does and how well he does it, to the level of diplomacy, where a man is assessed on his opinions, and on how he uses words to cloak them. I did not like the change and it was a source of worry to me.

With these thoughts in mind I drove at last up a long road lined with beech trees, and swung carefully into the driveway of Logie House. Why he was there, and not at Scone Palace, I never found out. No policeman jumped out of the shrubbery to close the gates when I had passed. No whistles sounded. The Earl was Lord Lieutenant of the County of Perth, and Convenor of the Police Committee of Perthshire County Council, and, as such, had all the forces of law and order, both civil and military, at his command. Daniel and the lions' den came to my mind as I drove on, but I felt instinctively that the estate was not bristling with detectives.

I pulled up in the courtyard in front of the house. In the darkness I could see little of it except that it was huge. Several lights burned out into the night, and a hospitable feeling came over me. I felt that it was indeed almost Hogmanay, and that preparations were afoot for its celebration.

I stood beside the car and finished a cigarette. I knew that the Earl had publicly embraced the cause of self-government, yet I could not be certain that he would also condone my interpretation of what had been necessary to focus our support. Earls are Earls, I thought, contradicting my earlier view, that they were but commoners with titles. Still, it was worth a try. Half the world will cross the road to lout at a Lord, and I had crossed two counties to do much the same. If he would give us some public encouragement, announce that our action, while unusual, was inspired purely by love of our country, and communicate the terms of the petition to His Majesty, he would be doing us a great service. Even if he did not openly commit himself, the fact that he was seeing me was of considerable value, for he was making himself some sort of accessory after the fact of a putative crime. Accessory after the fact was not a crime in Scotland, but, by not turning me in, he could face a charge of attempting to pervert the course of justice. To hell with striped trousers and the niceties of the law! I stubbed out my cigarette in the ash tray of the car and went forward and rapped loudly on the door.

The door was opened by someone whom I presumed to be the Countess of Mansfield. I did not introduce myself, for that would not have been true to the part I was playing, and indeed I had no intention of giving my name. I looked round the brightly lit hall, a homely enough place, if bigger than what I was used to. Only minutes before I had been lost in the cold and darkness. Now I had stepped from the wings onto the stage. I tried to think of it the way the Countess would be thinking of it, and smiled at her. I could be all sorts of a violent tough, for all she knew. I was the stranger out of the night who came and went and whose identity was as little known as that of the little folk themselves.

'I have an appointment with the Earl,' I said when the door had closed behind me.

The lady looked at me. 'You're late.' she said. It was more a query to establish my identity than a rebuke.

'I was due an hour ago,' I said. 'The roads were bad.'

I was led up a broad stairway and along a corridor from which doors opened on either side. The Earl was to receive me in his own room, for he had developed a heavy cold and was doctoring it in bed. The Countess showed me in and then withdrew.

It was a homely room in which I could feel at ease, and the reception I got from the Earl did nothing to erase my first impression.

'Don't tell me your name.' he said. 'It's better that I shouldn't know it.'

'That's just as it should be,' I agreed.

As I sat down, the Earl continued, 'And let me congratulate

you on one of the most brilliant exploits in Scottish history.'

This was laying it on a bit thick, but of course I was delighted. We had made many blunders. Many of our actions verged on the stupid, and success had been brought. to us by an enormous amount of luck. I knew that if the Earl was in possession of all the facts he could hardly describe the episode as brilliant. Still, it was the first praise I had had from anyone unconnected with me or the enterprise. Few men have defences against words like his, and I had none.

'Now tell me,' asked the Earl, 'are you a communist or a republican?'

I assured him that I was neither. Yet I had that strange feeling that it would not have made much difference if I had been. Here was a man who loved his country and everyone in it, whatever views they held. Yet the fact that I held much the same views as himself was no doubt of some reassurance to him. He had been afraid that I might be some form of extremist who would graduate from stone lifting to bomb throwing, but my support for the Covenant reassured him. You can do much more as a moderate than as an extremist. He too was a Covenanter, and he knew that there were no wild men in that movement.

At length I told him about the petition. He agreed that it was a good idea. There had been much speculation as to who was behind the whole affair, and what their aims could be. This would focus matters, and stop a lot of wild speculation. I produced it and read it to him. and he did not think that we should change a word of it.

But when I suggested that he might take it and act as our intermediary, he demurred. He pointed out that someone like him could not become too deeply involved in a plot like ours. Our action was for young unknowns, not for people of title, rank and position. I had to agree with him. I had come in out of the night, an unknown youth, with only verbal guarantees of my politics, and none at all of my sanity. The best I could hope for was a sympathetic hearing, but I could not realistically expect support. It would have been foolish for any public man at that time to have taken an active part in the exploit with people of whom he knew nothing. I had not mentioned John MacCormick's name, although I suspect that he thought that John had had a hand in it.

'Still,' continued the Earl, 'I may be able to help you. I may be able to let it be known that you have been to see me, and that I'm convinced that you're not wild men but moderate young people driven to anger at the way Westminster treats Scotland.'

This was no small service, as I realised, and I accepted the offer gratefully.

The Earl shifted about in his bed, and I could see that he still had something on his mind. On the bedclothes lay a copy of the *Bulletin* which contained the report of my telephone call from Newcastle, in which I had stated that the Stone was in Scotland. He looked uneasily at me, and then his curiosity got the better of him.

'I—er—don't want to know anything about it.' Then he burst out with a rush. 'But is it in Scotland yet? I've worked it out with maps and times, and I don't see how it could possibly have been got over the Border by the time it says here,' and he indicated the newspaper.

'No,' I said. 'That story was a decoy to let some of us get home.'

'It's not in the Serpentine?' he asked anxiously. Everyone wanted to know if the Stone was in the Serpentine. Why we should carefully remove it from Westminster Abbey and throw it into a puddle in a London park, Scotland Yard alone knew.

'No. It's not in the Serpentine,' I said.

He chuckled. 'You know you'll have to be careful,' he said. "They'll send you to prison when they catch you. The English don't like a joke against themselves, and you've twisted the lion's tail until it's come away in your hands.'

I thought to tell him that the Unicorn's horn was as sharp as the lion's teeth, but I decided to play it low key, and simply said, 'I know.'

As I rose to go he leant back and looked at the ceiling. 'Of course if the police ask if I have heard from you people, I shall have to say that you have been to see me.'

I was dismayed, for I had come to his house under safe-conduct, and I thought that in these days of scientific crime detection a safe conduct should also cover giving clues to the police. I looked at the decanter from which, at his invitation, I had recently poured myself a generous dram, and wondered if he would be annoyed if I wiped my prints off it.

'Well,' I said, my voice filled with dismay, 'if they ask for a description, I hope you'll just repeat the one that was given by the policeman outside the Abbey.'

He sat up sharply at that. 'Description!' he thundered. 'Description! I shall give them no description! I shall tell them that I am not an Argyll to betray a fellow countryman.'

We shook hands and I let myself out of his room, and found my way downstairs. The Countess, who had been waiting in the hall opened the door for me. I said good night and passed into the darkness. The door closed and I was once again alone.

I started the car and drove down the drive chuckling. What a delightful man! Not an Argyll indeed! That was a remark I could dine out on anywhere for years to come. Well almost anywhere, but not in Inveraray. No. Certainly not in Inveraray!

The petition still lay in my breast pocket, but my mission had not been entirely fruitless. I had made an ally, who, even if he would not play an active part, was quite clearly enchanted by the whole affair. We knew how ordinary people were thinking. Now I had seen an Earl's pennant fluttering in the wind. And the wind was coming from the same direction. On reflection it was really a very brave thing he had done, just to see me. After all, he was the Lord Lieutenant of the County, the King's representative, and he had done nothing to apprehend me. I felt certain that anything he said about us would be favourable. Even if he made no public announcement, his private conversation would help us. He moved in influential circles where there were public frowns at our action. A private chuckle or two would do no harm at all.

But I had still to get back to Glasgow to make my report, and to decide how best to get rid of the petition, which was still hanging like a penance round my neck. People in Scotland are always suggesting sending petitions to the sovereign. They should try to draft one themselves. Then they should start to wonder how to send it.

I found the road to Perth quite easily, and from there I telephoned Glasgow and asked them to arrange a council of war for my return. Then I had a cup of tea in a melancholy little cafe before I set off on the sixty mile journey. It was late when I arrived in Glasgow, for the roads were abominable. We met after midnight for the second night in succession in John MacCormick's flat at 5 Park Quadrant. The same four were present, Bill, Bertie Gray, and of course John MacCormick and myself.

I was anxious to get the proceedings over as quickly as possible for I was very tired. There was really very little to decide. The petition had to be issued quickly, for the public had to know what we were about. I had had doubts all along about the wording of it, but I had now been reassured by an outsider, the Earl, that it was impressive, although it still sounded high falutin nonsense to me. We decided that next day we would convey the petition directly to the Press. Bill undertook to type it out on his mother's typewriter, so that there would be no chance of handwriting experts tracing it back to its author. John also pointed out that, if we ever wished to issue a similar declaration, the use of the same typewriter would validate it as surely as a signature. Typescripts are unique to each typewriter. I saw Bill looking thoughtful at this. Privately, I held the view that there was no one else in Scotland with the style to frame such a document, and that that would be identification enough. John MacCormick himself was delightfully and naively unique.

Before I went off to bed there was one more matter to be settled. I wanted the petition to be sent out from Edinburgh, for I thought that we might bluff the police into concentrating their enquiries on that town. For the same reason the others wanted it to be sent out from Glasgow. The police, they contended, would expect us to leave it as far as possible from our own doorstep; if we left it in Edinburgh, the police would suspect Glasgow, and vice versa.

The Taking of the Stone of Destiny

The others were overestimating the forces against us. In actual fact the petition was left in a Glasgow newspaper office and it was on Glasgow that the police immediately concentrated their enquiries. Upon that circumstance no comment can be made.

Forty years on

I never met the Earl of Mansfield again. When I was called to the Bar just over three years later, I refused to take the oath of loyalty to the Sovereign in English form, and it was changed to its present style to accommodate me. I was the first advocate since the Union to insist on this. As a result my calling to the Bar occasioned much publicity.

The Earl must have read about it in the newspapers, for I had a charming little note from him, congratulating me, and wishing me well in my chosen career. Many years later when I read of his death it was like a personal loss, and although we had only had that one meeting I felt a sudden grief at his passing.

I move in circles where the aristocracy is either sneered at or fawned on. Any that I have met have seemed to me to be very ordinary people. It takes all types to make an Earl, just as it takes all types to make a commoner. Some good; some bastards. I am not prepared either to disparage or praise any Scot, or anyone else for that matter, because of the style of his birth. I don't know if the Earl of Mansfield did us any good, but he certainly didn't do us any harm. I do not believe that he who is not for us is against us. I do not accept that anyone who does not agree with me is a traitor to his country. Ach! But I cannot stomach class snobbery at all, especially middle class snobbery. There are only two classes, real people and puppets. I have little time for the latter, except to twitch their strings to watch them jump and jerk.

Chapter Twenty-Two

It was late when I awoke that Friday forenoon. It was the first full night's sleep I had had for a week. I felt great. I lay thinking of recent events. Seven days ago, following months of planning, and years of dreaming, we had left for London. The week had passed; water had flowed under bridges. Yet somehow we had triumphed over time. We had lived years of adventure in seven days. Into each day we had stuffed as many experiences as Santa Claus might stuff toys into a stocking. I felt older by much more than a week. It would be nice to relax and catch up with my social life. Life is for living.

My thoughts were broken by sounds outside my door. For a moment I thought it was the police, and started into careful wakefulness. Then I heard Alan's voice and knew that I was still safe. A knock came to the door and Gavin's voice made the room quiver.

'Come on! Come on! Come on! Can't lie in bed all day.' He beat thunderously on the door. I sighed and rose and let them in. They sat down and Alan gave me a cigarette. As we smoked I told them of the happenings of the last two days, and they agreed that the petition was an excellent idea.

As I spoke I could see that Alan had something on his mind. He was only giving half his attention to what I was saying, and he paced up and down the room like an uneasy animal, which was unlike his usual casual manner. He was solemn and silent until I had finished, and then he told me his trouble.

'My father's terribly worried about the Stone,' he said. 'He thinks that it will disintegrate if we don't do something about it soon.'

It appeared that after I had left him the previous morning his father had taken thought. Stuart and Stuart were a major civil engineering firm in the west of Scotland, so of course Mr Stuart knew a lot about stone. It occurred to him that any piece of sandstone which had lain for six centuries in a dry and constant atmosphere might have lost a great deal of its strength. If it were now exposed to the elements for any length of time, it might suck up water like blotting paper and split into fragments when the water froze.

This had not occurred to me. It seemed feasible enough, for ice can split stone. I sat on the edge of my bed and cupped my chin in my hands and thought how nice it would be to take a day off and have a casual lunchtime pint. That evening I had a long standing arrangement to take a girl out for dinner. I had had no social life for a fortnight. My dinner jacket was lying crumpled on the floor, and I had been stepping round it since I had last worn it a fortnight before at Daft Friday. I hadn't had time to hang it up. It would be nice to be normal again. Then I thought about the Stone lying in that wood, covered only by leaves and freezing soil, and of the hunt that was still on for it. If this information were accurate then we would have to get back on the road again.

But was it accurate? I had no means of knowing. If it was, I would have expected the police to issue a statement saying so. They would know that that would force us to take it out of hiding, and they would have their roadblocks out again everywhere. On the other hand, the police might not have the intelligence and knowledge that Mr Stuart had. And as Gavin painted a lurid picture of our going back for the Stone and having to shovel it into paper pokes, I sighed, and agreed that something had better be done.

While Allan went off to discuss the matter with his father I dressed and went over to the Union to tell Bill Craig of the new complication. We must now do everything in our power to preserve the Stone, and Allan must reassure Mr Stuart that this was being done. Mr Stuart was an unknown factor.

When I met Bill, he was inclined to treat the whole matter as a joke. He took me to the door of the Union and patted the wall. 'This is stone,' he said. 'It's sandstone. In the summer it's dry. In the winter it's wet. The rain falls on it. The frost freezes it. Yet the Union isn't falling down.'

I was more inclined to listen to Mr Stuart than to Bill, for while

Bill had the fluent tongue, Mr Stuart had the technical knowledge. There are a few occasions when knowledge is preferable to blarney, although as a law student I much prefer the latter. But this was a time for knowledge. I had arranged with Alan that we would meet his father outside the King's Theatre, and although Bill protested that he had much work to do, and that he was unshaven and tired, I dragged him down town to the meeting.

When we met Mr Stuart there was little doubt that he was very anxious. He put forward a strong *prima facie* case for the immediate recovery of the Stone. His sense of urgency transferred itself to me, and to Bill also, and we promised him that we would act immediately to recover the Stone, and bring it into a place of shelter from the elements. Meanwhile, Mr Stuart suggested that Alan should drive up to Ross-shire and discover from Kay where her piece of Stone was lying. He wanted reassurance that it was under cover. Bill and I made an appointment to meet Councillor Gray and John MacCormick that afternoon, and arranged that Gavin and Alan should keep in touch with us. Then we left Mr Stuart, full of worries for the slowly disintegrating Stone.

It was late that afternoon before John MacCormick, Bertie Gray, Bill and myself were able to get together. It was Friday, the last Friday in 1950, and the offices were closing down for the long weekend. Even in times of crisis ordinary things must go forward, and although Bill and I chafed at the delay we knew that there was nothing we could do to speed up the meeting. Finally, when the last figure had been totted up, and the last account paid, the four of us got together and I put the new situation before them.

At first Bertie Gray laughed at the idea of going down for the Stone that night. As a monumental sculptor he had worked with stone all his life, and the technical question of the Stone's safety came within the scope of his experience. It would take no hurt, he maintained. The meeting resolved into a contest between Bertie and myself. He pointed out that the police hunt was at its height, and that there was every likelihood of our car being stopped and searched as we crossed the Border. We had just come back from danger. 'Don't,' he pleaded, 'Don't go back down there again and take more risks. At least wait until the weather is better. More snow is forecast.'

I was not so sure. I did not want to find myself caught in the nip of two elderly experts, each contradicting the other. Even if the Stone were not in danger, Mr Stuart's belief that danger existed must be a factor in the equation. Anyway, it had to be brought back sometime. The police had been active right along the Border for five days now, and we had got through safely. They could not go on stopping cars for ever. By Sunday the Border would be open. Again, it was possible that Alan and I might be arrested at any moment, and it would be of considerable advantage if one or other of us were to accompany the expedition to fetch it back. After all, we had hidden it.

I advocated my case with some fluency, for my heart was in it. Anyone who has ever tasted adventure knows that it is the hardest thing in the world to sit still. Bertie's arguments were good, but Mr Stuart's were good too. Where there was a division of opinion, I was on the side of immediate action. In the back of my mind lurked the threat of impending arrest; and tucked away behind that was my own belief in myself. I suppose it was vanity, but I felt that if I was arrested everything might go to pigs and whistles. The Stone must be recovered before that happened. At last, when John MacCormick and Bill Craig had thrown their arguments onto my side of the scale, Bertie gave way. To this day he maintains that we took an unnecessary risk in going south that night, but he immediately started to organise our expedition.

There was one subject, however, on which the four of us were in complete harmony. We were all certain that Alan's projected trip north to Kay's home involved the taking of risks out of all proportion to any possible gain. Inverasdale is a small remote village, and very few cars would arrive there in the dead of winter. If Alan and Gavin paid a flying visit to Kay, people would talk. And none of us could afford to be kenspeckle figures at that time. Nor were we worried about the small piece of the Stone.

We knew that it was in the boot of the Anglia, in someone's garage, and that was the best place for it. We had no qualms about that.

As we had been talking about Alan's trip north, we had also been planning my trip south. Bertie Gray tried to insist that those of us who had been to London at Christmas should not go back again. We had tried our luck enough, and by now it must be wearing thin. Better to send a fresh team.

I laughed at his arguments. I had been in the affair from the beginning, and I was not going to be shouldered out of it now. To let someone else bring the Stone back was unthinkable. Who would he get? Eh? Was he going to go out into Sauchiehall Street, and shout, 'Hi, Jimmy. C'mere a minute? Gonna go down and bring us the Stone?' What was wrong with me anyway? Who else could do it better than me? Eh?

We nearly had a face to face argument about it, because I don't think he was used to being laughed at, but his idea was absurd, and I saw John MacCormick turn away to hide a smile. I was, however, prepared to concede Bertie's point to the extent of taking a new team apart from myself. I felt it unfair to expose Alan and Gavin to further risks. Alan especially. He was much younger than I was and we had not had all that much rest in these last seven days. Bill was his natural stand-in, and he had assumed all that evening that he would be called upon to go. There was of course no one better qualified than himself. Although he could not drive, he excelled at all human relationships. The occasion was soon to arise when this excellence was to be put to the test.

Simultaneously, Bill and I thought of our third man. John Josselyn was an Englishman by birth, and the son of a Rear Admiral, but he had been educated in Scotland and had come to regard himself as one of us. We certainly so regarded him. He had arrived for Hogmanay from Bath in Somerset where he was employed in the Admiralty in some frightfully hush hush work on submarines. Trust the Admiralty to have their submarine section on a trickle of a river. Bill immediately set out to recruit him. He found him drinking coffee in the Union and approached him quietly.

John Josselyn was the most spectacular of all the people who concerned themselves with the Stone. Like the rest of us, he was small in stature. He had tiny twinkling seaman's eyes, and from his chin jutted a rough and glorious beard, which stuck before him as though its ends had been heated red hot and hammered into shape on an anvil. His enemies, and they were many, hated him and would have killed him; his friends, and they were legion, would have died for him; he himself lived in a world of his own, cherishing the bizarre and deriding the commonplace. He never did a moderate thing in his life, and I loved him like a brother.

His recruitment must be the shortest contract on record.

'Are you doing anything over New Year?' Bill asked.

'Aye!' said Joss. He loved to affect Scots speech. 'A'm going up to Mull.'

'Would you not rather come south to bring back the Stone of Destiny?' asked Bill.

'Aye!' said Joss. 'A would that.'

Back in Bertie Gray's office we were having great difficulty in getting hold of a car. His own car was of little use, for it had gone sour with age, and could not be expected to stand up to a thousand mile non-stop trip. It was too late to hire one, as the garages would all be closed for the holiday, and there was no one else in the plot who owned a car. Cars were not all that common. Had we told what we wanted one for, we could have had a whole fleet of them, but telling was a risk we could not idly take. Too many people knew already. Again our minds turned to Alan Stuart.

He was at that moment provisioning a car for the trip north to see Kay, the trip we all looked on with so much misgiving. We had hoped that we should not again have to call on his family's generosity, but it seemed that there was to be no other way, so we telephoned him at his house. He was just leaving as our call came through, and he assured us that he would be with us in half an hour.

While we were waiting for him, Bill returned to report his

successful interview with John Josselyn. There was only one drawback. Joss could not drive. That meant I would be expected to drive all the way non-stop. A thousand miles at an average speed of twenty five or thirty miles an hour. The arithmetic lost me, but whatever the result it was too much. I would have to set aside all my cautious thoughts about Alan. Alan would have to come.

Shortly afterwards, Alan himself arrived. He saw the arguments that it might endanger Kay if he went north. He was a little more reluctant to go south. He would have gone to the South Pole to get the Stone. It was the car he was worried about. Already he had 'mislaid' one of the family cars. The Anglia was hidden in some garage in Birmingham, and his father had had every right to read the Riot Act and had not done so. Now Alan was being asked to take a much more expensive car, a fourteen horse power Armstrong-Siddeley, and dash fiercely over icy roads with a snow warning out, and all Scotland Yard's bloodhounds howling behind. It was his choice.

Being Alan he chose the dangerous course, risked the car and his father's wrath, and brought the Stone home. On this trip, fear of his father was a very real thing with Alan. And while I am certain that both he and his father will look back on that fear and smile, it was no laughing matter at the time. When we returned with the Stone, Alan was torn between the need to tell his father that all was well with the Stone, and the desire not to tell him how all had become well. In the end all was forgiven, but we pushed Mr Stuart's generosity to the limit.

Little now remained to be done. Bill and I had dined amply off fish and chips, and the car was provisioned with food and flasks of hot drink. Joss was waiting in my lodgings. We had enough money to cover most contingencies; we had road maps; we now had a car. Plans we had none, for we had no time to make them. Our operation was simple. We had to bring the Stone back. The lack of any definite plan was no drawback. We did not know what we would have to meet, but our arrangements were flexible, and we could mould them to meet any situation.

Bertie went off to deliver our petition to the Press. There was one of us who was glad to see the back of it, and that one was me. After that he and John could only wait in anxiety, while once again we set off south.

Forty years on
I had no option, had I?

I forgot to make my excuses to my dining companion of the night, and stood her up, poor girl. When I came back I telephoned her and told her I had been away south bringing back the Stone of Destiny. She was not amused. She was even less amused when she learned some months later that I had told her the truth. She never spoke to me again.

Chapter Twenty Three

After the old Ford, the Armstrong-Siddeley was the last word in comfort. It was frightfully well-bred; not quite out of the top drawer, but getting on that way. It held the doubtful roads well, the steering didn't have three inches of play in it, the doors and windows fitted so that it was draught proof, and, above all, it had a heater. After the gusty winds and freezing cold of the Ford, it was bliss. John Josselyn and Bill Craig had the best of it. They did not suffer the cold we first four had endured.

Joss was waiting in my room, and was very pleased to see us when we picked him up. He had been waiting so long that he was beginning to think that it was some elaborate practical joke, but when we assured him that it was no joke and that we were going to start immediately, his eyes sparkled, and he was silent for joy, the only time I ever knew him to be without a word. He just could not believe it.

Bill had given him only a few of the details, and while we filled in the blanks for him, I rushed round the room and packed all my available grips and haversacks with a miscellaneous collection of shirts, socks and suits. It occurred to me that now that we were travelling in style, we had better have the impedimenta of style, so in went my dinner jacket too. It might help to convince any police patrol that we were what we claimed to be. What precisely that was going to be would have to fit the circumstances of the time.

We had now only one call to make, and we proceeded to make it as quickly as possible. Gavin was still under the impression that he was accompanying Alan north on the trip to Inverasdale, and it was necessary to call at his lodgings to tell him that this trip was cancelled.

I could see that both Bill and Johnny were worried, and I knew what was on their minds. Only four could go on the trip south, and they both felt that Gavin had a better title to be one of the four than either of them had. Gavin had been one of the first four, and he was a driver. We sent Bill in to speak to Gavin and waited in the car for his return. No doubt Johnny felt that as last comer he was likely to be the one to be jettisoned, and as a particular friend I felt for him. Bill returned with Gavin, who had agreed not to insist on his right to come with us. He wished us luck and told us to ca' canny. Alan let in the clutch, and we set off on our second adventure.

It was not a happy night for driving. The sky was overcast with cloud, and although the temperature had risen considerably the roads were still ice bound. There was every indication that we would get snow before morning. However, we were in fine spirits. If to travel hopefully is better than to arrive, setting off on a journey is better still. I do not believe that pleasures are stronger in anticipation than in realisation. That is a philosophy of the defeated. The tremendous rush of preparation is to be borne only as a means to the gusty appreciation of the result. We were again tasting result. We were travelling south to bring back the Stone of Destiny.

We all enjoyed each other's company. Johnny sang what he said was a Gaelic song, although he had not a word of that language, and I recited 'Edinbane'. Then we sat and talked about the police and what fools they were making of themselves. If they were no cleverer than they appeared to be, we should have no trouble. And so the hours passed. We sang our way southwards, and all the world was young.

Yet as we wore the heel out of the night we sang less and less. A thousand miles is a long way non stop, and we had no intention of stopping. Finally we paired off; one driver accompanied by a talker, whose job was to keep the driver from falling asleep. Bill was my partner, and we talked about many things as the headlights cut swathes in the icy darkness and the snow crunched under the wheels. Bill had a degree in history, and was due to sit his finals in economics that spring. He had many new ideas about the Scotland we would build when we had taken control of our own destiny

166

into our own hands, and ceased to permit our nearest neighbour to grow weeds in our garden. Remember that we were still intoxicated with success. We were young. We believed that our actions had taken Scotland a long way along the road she must one day travel to the end.

At Carlisle we stopped and filled the car with petrol, for although it was powerful, it also had a great thirst. One of our fellow students lived near here, and we determined to call on him. His father was a doctor with a country practice so he travelled a lot over the Border roads. He would know what police patrols were out, and whether or not it would be possible to slip through them unobserved.

We had some difficulty in finding the house, and finally we stopped and Bill put through a telephone call, so that when we eventually arrived our friend was waiting for us on his doorstep. Johnny, Alan and I sat in the car while Bill went out. The student was thoroughly trustworthy, but it was fairer to him as well as to us, to let him know as little as possible. He was a friend of Bill's, and Bill alone need deal with him.

In a short time Bill returned to report that all was well. Police activity had slackened in the area and there was every chance that we would get through. The road from Longtown to Langholm seemed the best bet, for it was one used much by local people and little by long distance traffic. Our friend was certain that if we crossed the Border there, we would not be stopped. To make doubly certain, Bill had arranged one of his code signals to be used if we were in any doubt. We were to telephone this man and ask him how his auntie was keeping. If the roads were clear, his auntie was well; if they were completely infested with police his auntie was very ill; gradations in her health between these two states would indicate how active the police were being. Fortunately the police kept within doors that weekend, so our friend's holiday was not clouded by family sickness. We drove south from Carlisle knowing that our intelligence arrangements were in good hands.

Our trip from Penrith over the Pennines to Scotch Corner was

167

less eventful than when we had travelled in the Ford. True, there had been a heavy snowfall, but the wheels of much traffic had hammered it flat. Although we skidded occasionally and had much wheel spin we were never in danger. If the roads were no worse than this we would make good time.

Up on the roof of England we halted to stretch our legs. The sky was overcast but a hazy glow came through from the lowland towns. Darkness is a decreasing phenomena. On all sides stretched a measureless waste of snow, which shone wan and uneasy under a clouded sky . There was complete silence, except only for the crackle of the ice under our feet. We were frightened a little as though something was watching us, and we were glad when we piled into the car again and closed the doors against the cold mystery of the moor.

We continued to make good speed. Alan and I changed with each other fairly frequently so we did not tire. We ate hugely of the store of food which was in the car, and looked longingly at the gill of whisky which Alan's father had given him; but we did not drink it. We were preserving it for a special occasion. Of sleep we had little, for both Johnny and Bill were fresh and their remarks lit the night with humour. Time and again, when sleep was almost there, laughter would come and destroy it. We did not mind. We were making good time. It was a time to laugh.

We stopped at Doncaster for a cup of tea. It was still early morning but the cafe was thronged with football fans on their way by bus to a game. They had early morning papers, and were talking more about the Stone than about football. *Ruat coelum!* If we were ousting football from its proper place the world was swinging off its axis. We buttoned up our accents, and asked for tea and rolls in monosyllables, and urged Johnny to do most of the talking; but our ears were open and we were delighted to note the interest our actions had aroused.

Dawn had scarcely begun to show itself when the first flurry of snow swept across the headlights, blotting out the way ahead. At first the only hindrance was to visibility; each snowflake was a reflector which turned the headlights back into the eyes of the driver. Soon we were reduced to a crawl by our inability to see. Carried by the wind, the tiny snowflakes slid across the road until they found a hollow to lie in. In half an hour the drifts were several inches deep and the back wheels began to skate and spin. Snow built up under the mudguards and tore at the wheels. When dawn broke, and the snow was still falling, we knew that we were going to have to find a garage and have chains fitted. Outside Newark we stopped to pick up a lassie with a shopping basket who was waiting in the snow, hoping her bus was still running, and she was able to direct us to a garage where we would get good attention.

We found this under the shadow of Newark Castle. The mechanic assured us that he could attend to our wants, so we left the car in his charge. It was now coming on for ten o'clock and the nearby hotel rather brusquely refused us breakfast, so we had a wash and shave in their toilet, and left under a barrage of frowns. We were still hungry, and on enquiry were directed to a small eating house full of stuffed birds and filth, where we had the worst breakfast in England for which we were charged the ruinous price of three and sixpence each.

For the last few hours we had held constant discussions on the best place to stow the Stone in the car. Underneath the boot there was a receptacle for the spare wheel, and it seemed to me that, if the Stone would fit in there, it would be an ideal hiding place. We had some argument on the subject, and to settle the matter once and for all I bought a ruler to measure it. Then we discovered that none of us could remember the measurements of the Stone, so we had to buy a morning paper to find out. The papers contained a very full description of the Stone, including the exact measurements. I do not know if this description ever assisted anyone else, but it certainly proved invaluable to us.

The car was now ready and we went to collect it. The chains swallowed up a fair proportion of our fast dwindling money. We found, however, that it was worth it. Although the snow had stopped falling it still lay deeply, and indeed we heard later that the roads we had travelled were classed by the motoring associations as impassable. It was not until we were well south of Stamford that we could stop to take the chains off.

This was now my opportunity to stop and measure the spare wheel aperture, and to my intense chagrin it was, as all the others had maintained, too small. It seemed that there was no alternative but to put the Stone in the boot. I did not like this. If the police stopped us, that would be the first place they would look. I wanted to have a chance to bluff it out even if we were stopped.

I checked over the car and discovered that the front passenger seat was separate from its backrest. The seat could be lifted out, springs, upholstery and all. We moved the backrest to the limit of its travel and removed the seat, measured the space carefully, and discovered that there was ample room for the Stone. True, the passenger would be uncomfortable. He would have to sit with his legs straight in front of him, but with a travelling rug over the Stone, and a coat over his knees, nothing would be visible unless the nearside door was opened. We would have to keep it locked.

At Letchworth we stopped, and Johnny and I got out to search for a travelling rug to cover the Stone in its new capacity of a car seat. The travelling rugs were more than we could afford, and we had to make do with a second-hand coat. Thus the Stone of Destiny came back to Scotland, clad not in the purple of Kings, but covered humbly with a commoner's cast-off overcoat.

It was growing dark when we arrived in London, but we were very cheerful. It had taken us twenty four hours to cover four hundred miles, but we had kept ourselves fresh for the night's work which lay ahead of us. We had plenty of time, for we did not wish to arrive at Rochester until late in the evening; the later we were, the fewer people there would be abroad. We headed for the West End and parked the car in the Strand. It will be remembered that on Christmas morning Bill had wired ten pounds to Gavin at the Strand Post Office. Gavin had returned to Glasgow and this money had never been uplifted. We determined to retrieve it now. Bill went into the Post Office, presented proof of Gavin's identity, signed Gavin's name and collected the money. Thus we added forgery to our many other heinous offences.

We bought papers and proceeded to a cafe to read them and to have a meal. The *STAR* carried a headline, *STONE: ARRESTS EXPECTED SOON.* We laughed a little uneasily about this. It seemed a long time since we had left Scotland, and we wondered if there had been any new developments. Then we read on and found that the police were still dredging all adjacent stretches of water. It seemed a cold pastime for that season of the year.

Towards 8.00 p.m. we took the road to Rochester. Alan and I had lost ourselves so often on this road that we had little hope of finding it first time. London is not so much a city as a desert of houses crowded together. Outside the West End there is no character whatsoever, only an unvarying monotony of houses. I am sure that it is easier to be lonely in London than anywhere else on earth. Certainly it is a featureless wilderness to the comparative stranger. This time, however, we were lucky, and in an amazingly short time we were passing the familiar Elizabethan roadhouse and shooting along the avenue of poplars.

It was a dark night but not too dark for our purpose. The snow had not reached as far south as this, but there was a hint of it in the air. The temperature was a few degrees below freezing point, and occasionally the back wheels swung across a patch of ice. The weather seemed to have frightened most motorists indoors for we were agreeably surprised to find the road almost deserted. We were getting close to the hiding place.

One after another, in the grey of the night, Alan and I picked up our landmarks. First there was the little cart track beside which the Stone had lain hidden on Christmas day. Then a few miles further on there was the line of bushes into which we had tipped it in the vain hope that they would be sufficient to conceal it. Soon, against the dark backdrop of the sky, we saw the outline of the aircraft hangars. We swept past a line of trees before which a dancing fire cast shadows on a gypsy's caravan.

'We're nearly there,' I said.

Johnny chuckled with delight. 'Wouldn't it be funny,' he laughed, 'if the gypsies were camping on top of the Stone?' He had scarcely finished speaking when the outskirts of Rochester reached out to meet us.

I said nothing. I was suddenly afraid. My excitement was mounting. The chances were a million to one against it. Such a thing was too extraordinary to happen. Johnny fell silent. He too knew what I was thinking.

We turned the car and as we passed the pub, we checked the mileage on the speedometer. I watched the tenths of a mile clicking up. The Stone was two and a half miles distant. At the two mile mark the fire came into sight. The gypsies were going to be near enough to be difficult. As the fifth tenth came up, we passed the fire and the caravan. There was no doubt about it. The gypsies, if gypsies they were, were camping directly on top of the Stone.

We had travelled almost five hundred miles. We were the most sought after people in Britain; the Stone might at this moment be cracking with frost. Yet our journey had been in vain. The Stone was guarded as surely as if it were back in Westminster Abbey.

Forty years on
Fate seemed determined to favour us with the picturesque.

Chapter Twenty Four

We drove two hundred yards up the road and stopped the car. This last stroke of ill luck was harder to bear than anything which had previously happened. We had, in the beginning, asked only for an even chance, and luck had joined us as the fifth man. We had accepted that, given thanks for it and relied upon it. Now the fifth man seemed to have joined the millions who were against us. It was so unexpected that it was cruel. The easy operation suddenly became one of great hazard. We discussed what we should do.

'Wait for twenty four hours,' I counselled. 'They can't stay here forever. We'd be fools to lose it now because we were too impatient to wait.'

'Ach,' said Johnny, the thruster. 'Walk through them and take it.' He wasn't going to be kept from the Stone by a wheen of gypsies.

We discussed ways and means. It would be impossible to outflank them and carry the Stone through the wood. They were just too close to it for any such attempt. We thought of impersonating a Squire and ordering them off, but they would probably have made us foolish by refusing to go. It would be useless to wait for them to go to sleep for the barking of their dogs would arouse them.

'Buy some bottles of whisky and get them drunk,' suggested Johnny again, but we dismissed this idea, for they might fight in drink, and none of us wanted to take on a drunken gypsy.

'What if they're detectives?' said Alan, voicing the fear which was in all our minds. Were the police not as stupid as their actions seemed to prove? Had they perhaps discovered the Stone. Was all their search in the puddles of England just a blind, while the modern Holmes sat on the Stone and played a gypsy fiddle? We discussed this seriously for a moment, for the situation was so fantastic that anything might be the key to it. Then we dissolved in laughter when we saw the fantasy of it. We decided that the police were as stupid as they looked.

Our laughter revived our drooping spirits. Bill got out of the car. 'I'll talk to them,' he said, 'and see what can be done.' I got out with him, and together we walked down towards the fire, our feet catching and tripping in the rough frozen grass of the roadside balk. The other two sat and waited.

I had often listened to Bill talk, both in public and private. I had heard him again and again in the riposte of argument, when two hard minds meet and strike sparks from each other. I had every confidence in his ability, but he was meeting a situation that was outside the ambit of ordinary experience.

As we drew nearer, we noticed that there were two caravans and two fires. It was the first one that we were interested in, for the blind back of the second one effectively screened the gypsies at the second fire from the hiding place.

In the leaping flames we could see an ancient gypsy couple sprawled against the fence, their boots outstretched to the blaze. The man could have put his hand through the fence and touched the Stone. Their caravan beetled over them, and the firelight fell across the black entrance. It was open and sinister. The trees leaned uneasily to the warmth, and the sparks rose through their bare branches like fireflies, and the darkness pressed around as though jealous of the fire. A lurcher pup came at us, jumping and fawning, and was called off by the woman. We came close to the fire.

'Can we have a heat at your fire?' Bill asked like a cheery traveller out of the night. The woman invited us in with a 'Sir,' and a smile. I said nothing. We sat silent for a long time. The firelight danced across the bronze faces of the gypsies in the frosty night. Then Bill started to talk.

He talked of the cold at first, and the woman nodded and smiled. He did not go hurriedly and there were many long pauses. Then he asked them how long they were staying and the woman said, 'For a day or two.' At this the man mentioned that it was late, and the hint was obvious.

Then Bill started talking in earnest while the flames leapt across our faces and the sparks shot up and the lurcher pup crept close to be fondled.

He talked first of all about the gypsies and how they were harried by the authorities. He talked about the free life they lived and how in these times there were many people who talked about liberty, and many more who soiled it by denying it to those whom they did not understand. He told them about our country in the north which was a little country, and which like the gypsies was striving to preserve its liberty and be itself. Their ways and customs were not ours, but the problem was the same all over the world. Darkness was coming down on the world and only a few people like the gypsies and the Scots foresaw that darkness and tried to live their lives like a light. The gypsies made no sound and no movement.

I watched Bill's face, young and earnest in the firelight. I can see it to this day. He had forgotten that he was playing a game, which was as well, for the gypsies would not have understood a game; they may not even have understood his words, but he was down beyond words to the level of sincerity, and they knew and trusted that.

Then he talked about liberty itself, and how in the end of the day it is the only precious thing. The slaves who would not be free, because their masters fed and clothed them, were still with us today, but food and drink vanished and left in the end only freedom or slavery. Freedom could be preserved, not in caravans or in houses, but only in people's hearts, and as soon as they stopped valuing it it disappeared. 'We're not like that,' he ended. 'And to keep our freedom we need something out of that wood. It's not wrong, but it's illegal. We are doing right, but we will go to jail if we're caught.' He looked at the gypsy simply and with no defiance.

The gypsy who had as yet scarcely spoken answered him.

'You can't get it just now,' he said without moving. 'There's a local man who isn't a gypsy at the next fire and you can't trust him.'

For a long time we followed the gypsy philosophy of staring into the fire as though it contained all wisdom and all knowledge. Then the outside world broke in in the shape of Alan and Johnny. They pulled the car up by the edge of the road and walked over to see what kept us so long. The gypsy woman looked up with patient serenity, and the lurcher bounded to meet them.

'They are our friends,' said Bill, and the gypsy smiled.

'Where is the Lia Fail?' whispered Johnny fiercely, using probably the only two Gaelic words he knew. Bill and I answered nothing, and soon all six of us sat staring silently at the fire.

In a little while, another gypsy drifted in from the group beyond the other caravan to see, no doubt, who had visited his friends. The two men talked for a little in their own language, and then the newcomer went back to his own fire.

'It will be all right,' said the gypsy. 'The stranger will be gone soon.'

Shortly afterwards a man came from the direction of the other fire. He mounted his bike and road off down the road towards Rochester. The gypsy from the other fire came back and told us it was safe.

My excitement uncoiled like a spring and I vaulted the fence. Alan followed with the torch. The Stone was exactly as we had left it. The litter on top of it was frozen stiff and came off in one piece like the lid of a box. It had protected the Stone, and the frost had hardly touched it. The four of us manhandled it up the slope and under the bottom bar of the railing.

When the gypsies saw the weight we were carrying, the two men rushed to our assistance. We carried it bodily across the grass and sat it in the space already prepared for it at the near side front seat. Alan and Johnny tumbled in. 'Go on and wait for us up the road,' said Bill and we returned to the fire.

I fumbled in my pocket and produced three pounds. I offered it to one of the gypsies. 'No!' he said. 'No!'

The Taking of the Stone of Destiny

I felt despicable. In my country I would not have done it, but I had judged my hosts by the Londoners. 'Yes!' I cried, to cover up my shame, and thrust the money at him. I had violated one of the most sacred rules of hospitality, and shown myself unworthy to sit by their fire. Feeling like a commoner among kings, I thanked them for their hospitality, and together Bill and I left the circle of warmth and kindness and stepped back into the cold and the namelessness of the darkness.

I do not know if the gypsies knew what they did that night. I like to think that they did. The Stone has a long strange unknown history, and gypsies may have played a part in that history before that night. It is difficult, after that episode, to deny that there is a design in life, although what that design is I have never known. The gypsies were no handicap to us. It was only in our bitterness when we first saw them that we lost our faith, and swore that there were never people as unlucky as we.

How long had they been there? I do not know. How long did they stay after we had gone? I do not know that either. But I do know that as long as they were there they were the most efficient guard we could have placed on the Stone. Who would be suspicious of a car stopped at a gypsy's caravan? Who would look for the Stone of Destiny in the heart of a gypsy encampment in the English countryside? Yet the police looked in many places at that time and there were many who would have been suspicious had they seen something carried into a car from a lonely and deserted wood near London.

Sometimes I wonder if they were really there, yet they must have been, for we all saw and spoke to them. But why? Out of all the broad acres and highways and lanes of England, why on that exact spot? Within one yard? Why on that exact night of all nights? Must everything be explained? If so, I fail. As we walked up towards the car Bill turned to me and said:

'By God! The gypsies will have a fine place in the new Scotland we're going to build.'

'By God,' I said. 'They will.'

The Taking of the Stone of Destiny

Forty years on

My life has been full of coincidences, so full that I deny all theories of mathematical probability. Yet the coincidence of the gypsies is one of the most remarkable. People may draw conclusions if they wish. I can draw none. I only record the facts.

But one fact remains with me to this day with searing shame, and that is that I tried to repay kindness with money.

Chapter Twenty Five

A hundred yards up the road the car was waiting for us, and putting the gypsies out of our minds we saw the Stone and leapt in. The Stone was damp and earthy and as yet uncovered with any coat, but Johnny was sitting on it, his beard bristling and his eyes flashing with fierce pride.

'It's not groaning,' he said. 'I can't be a king.' The old legend has it that the Stone groaned aloud when the true king of Scots sat on it.

Half a mile from where we had left the gypsies, a road led off to the left. We dropped Bill at the corner and turned into it to make adjustments to the Stone. Bill would watch the main road and see whether the police swooped on the gypsies' camp. Someone might have seen us and reported the suspicious circumstances. We could take no chances.

As we manoeuvred the Stone into its most effective position Alan and I continued our argument. He was still certain that the boot was the best place for it, but I would not hear of it. We shoved and pulled at the Stone, until I was satisfied. It was not perfect, but it was as good as we were likely to get. In the dark, little was obvious, but by daybreak we would be nearing the Border, which was the place of greatest danger. From the road, Johnny appeared to be the right height, and it was not until the driving door was opened that he seemed to be at all awkward. Even then, with a coat over his legs he was natural enough. It was only when the nearside door was open that it could be seen that the seat had been removed and something substituted.

That seat was our biggest worry. If a patrol stopped us an intelligent constable might wonder where it had come from. We tried to lock it in the boot, but even there it would be noticeable, and anyway it was too big to go in. There was nothing for it but to leave it lying on the back seat. We draped it with coats and tried to make it look as much like an armrest as possible. But we were uneasy about it.

'We'll send somebody up by train with it,' I said.

I could feel Johnny studiously trying not to hear me. He knew that that would be his job, and he wanted to cross the Border with the Stone like the rest of us.

We picked Bill up at the corner. He had nothing to report, so we pointed the bonnet for London. We pulled away slowly. We had started on the last lap. I drove first and let Alan sleep. He would need all the rest he could possibly sandwich between his spells at the wheel. We would be tired before we reached Scotland. Yet as we gently cruised into the heart of London I was burning with excitement. The newsboys were still shouting the headlines, STONE: ARREST EXPECTED SOON. People were buying the papers and reading and wondering where it could be, while the Stone passed by, half a yard away. We looked out at them, and knew. It would be in Scotland tomorrow.

We passed through London without a word being said about the car seat. We had all remembered it, but we had all refrained from mentioning it. We were learning. It had been a mistake for the three of us to separate on Christmas Day. People work better together. The problem of the seat could wait until we were nearer the Border. In actual fact we took little risk. We reckoned that by that time, six days after the removal of the Stone, any police patrols would be confined to the Northern Counties of England. Time enough to take precautions when we were two hundred miles north of London.

As we drove, we discussed the best route to take. I had ridden them all on my powerful Speed Twin motorcycle when I was in the forces. The Great North Road was our easiest way, and the one least likely to be blocked with snow, but that road would be well watched. The same would apply to the A6 through Derby and Manchester. Furthermore, north of Lancaster this road climbs up over Shap, and there was a considerable chance that it would be impassable.

It seemed that our best route was to start by the A6. We

would go straight up through the heart of England to Nottingham, passing Luton, Bedford and Leicester on the way. From Nottingham we would head for York, crossing the Great North Road just south of Bawtry and passing thereafter through Snaith and Selby.

This was not our most direct route, but it had the advantage of keeping us to the secondary trunk roads, which were not so busy as to be carefully watched, but busy enough not to be blocked with snow. Having made our decision we wasted no further mental energy on argument. Alan and Johnny slept. I drove, and Bill read the map for me.

All the way to Luton we waited for the snow to fall. The night was dark and woolly, with the relaxed feeling in the air which is brought by the threat of snow. The weather seems to sigh, before expiring in whiteness. Luton brought the first snow flurries. Soon it fell in a steady white sheet. I was dazzled. The speedometer fell back, and we were reduced to a crawl. My eyes ached with peering through the snow, which seemed to be coming in handfuls, thrown at our tired eyes.

There was no doubt as to whether it would lie or not. It was soon binding under the mud-guards, and even on slight hills the engine whined and the rear end swung as the wheels failed to grip the road. We put off the evil hour of getting out into the cold to fit the chains to the rear wheels, but as we neared Bedford we knew that it was unavoidable. Outside, it was dark and cold and wet. The darkness pressed on us. The snow fell with that dull sound, which is like intensified silence. It was like an army creeping into position. I at least, was frightened, but we needed these chains.

We took them from the boot, unfankled them with many curses, and stretched them out on the snow. Then I carefully backed the car on to them. For fully half an hour we lay on the snow, while filth dripped on us from the mudguards and the wet crept into our skin. We wrestled and pulled at the reluctant freezing metal until our arms ached and our knuckles seemed red raw. What the garage man had easily accomplished was beyond our power. The ends of the chain obstinately refused to meet. We pulled and swore and twisted and finally gave up. We would have to try to drive without them.

We drove on. We could do nothing else. And all the time we were thinking of the bloody mush the Stone would make if we overturned and it thumped on top of us. But gradually we forgot our fears, and remembered only our successes. Each mile that came up on the clock was yet another mile nearer home. Even if we were finished now, every mile was a victory. And when occasionally, in our tiredness, we wondered if we were not straining ourselves in vain, we would pull the coat back from the Stone and rub our hands against its dear roughness.

And straining we were. We found an all night garage in the centre of Leicester. As we approached it Bill said to me:

'Give the wheel to Alan. You've been talking so slowly this while back that I can hardly make you out.'

I did not argue. When we had filled up, I tumbled into the back seat and went contentedly to sleep. I felt I had earned it. When I awakened, it was almost dawn. I asked where we were, and to my delight was told that we were only twenty miles from York. We had come an amazing distance. The snow had now stopped and when dawn had bleached the shadows we stepped out into a morning, fresh and clear and brilliant. The country undulated into the distance, virgin white and clean. The air smelt new. The sky was blue, the trees glittered with a rind of snow on all the branches. From further down the road came the roar of a tractor. It was the country, the beautiful country. When we had washed in the snow, we pushed on, furrowing the smooth road with our wheels. Soon we were in York, quiet and deserted in the Sabbath calm.

York was the place to say goodbye to Johnny and the car seat. We could bear the risk of it no longer. He was reluctant to go, but saw the necessity. We pulled up to let him off at a fork in the road in the northern outskirts of York. He wished us luck, and climbed out, taking the seat with him. His trip north was not free from events. He stood watching the wisp of steam from our exhaust as we vanished up the sunlit snowy road, and then turned away to find himself face to face with a policeman. We had let him off at the door of a brick built building which turned out to be a police box, and hearing the car a constable had come out.

'Good morning,' said Johnny politely.

The constable eyed him suspiciously. He was not used to seeing young men carrying car seats through York on Sunday mornings.

'Where are *you* going?' he asked; the sort of bloody stupid question to which there should be only two words in reply, although it is not wise to use them.

'Mull,' replied Johnny, shifting the seat from one hand to the other. The policeman did not seem to have heard of Mull. It was not on his beat. He scratched his head.

'And what are you doing with that car seat?' he asked. It was all very suspicious. It might be a stolen car seat.

'I'm taking it to Mull to people who need a new seat for their car,' Johnny explained patiently. 'A pig crapped on the other one.'

The policeman thought that one over. Well! Perhaps it was all in order. Johnny's accent was not that of a criminal. There was no law yet which forbade people to carry car seats through the streets. What could a poor constable do if Parliament refused to forbid the things that people did? Johnny walked off, watched by the constable.

Johnny caught a train to Newcastle on the first leg of his journey to Mull. At Newcastle, he found he had all afternoon to wait for a connection, so he passed the time by calling on a mutual friend of his and mine, who lived in Sunderland. She had known nothing of our plot, although she had immediately thought of me when she heard that the Stone had vanished. When she saw Johnny nonchalantly swinging the car seat everything became abundantly clear to her. She was not impressed. A great verbal storm broke over him. He was a fool. He would lose his job. He would go to prison. Ian Hamilton was a worthless lout who got everyone he met into trouble. Three years later I married that young woman. She is the mother of three of my four children.

While Johnny was getting my character reference in Sunderland, we three were driving steadily onwards. Here and there we picked up a hitch hiker, because the busses did not seem to be running. The hitch hiker sat in the back seat, while Bill sat in the front on the Stone. With them we talked gravely about current events, particularly the one which was in the headlines. Acting irony is better even than speaking it. With such incidents we enlivened the drive north.

We were again in need of petrol and we stopped at the Croft Hotel, only to be told that the pumps were closed. However, we were able to purchase some Sunday papers, so, forgetting the worry about getting fuel in the joys of the newspapers we continued on our way. As we crossed the Tees, Bill sat in the front seat and read out titbits. The front pages were full of us, and there were very learned and heavy articles inside. The heavier the newspaper, the heavier were the frowns and thunderings against us. Yet it was official England that was outraged, and I sensed among the ordinary people a huge delight at deflated pomposity. Bill read on.

"Look at this,' he suddenly cried in delight.

I took my eye for an instant from the road and glanced at the banner headline he was holding up. It read, STONE: £1,000 REWARD. I had never had as much money as that in my life. I wondered if I could surrender myself and claim it. That amount of money could buy a house. Yet a funny thing happened to that reward. Next week the offer was withdrawn. Not only was the paper boycotted in Scotland, but there was such strong protest in England at the idea of a newspaper offering blood money, that the circulation managers insisted that the editorial policy of the paper be changed. The people of England (who, according to Chesterton, have not spoken yet) were speaking out. In our favour.

We filled up at a garage at Salutation Corner on the south-west outskirts of Darlington, and as the garage attendant came to serve us I thought of that thousand pounds. Perhaps it was in his mind also. When he heard my accent he said, 'Scots? You haven't got the Stone of Destiny with you?'

'It's in the boot,' I quipped back and we both laughed.

'The police have been round asking what Scotsmen I've given petrol to,' he added. 'When they come back I'll tell them it went through this morning.'

We exchanged chuckles and I drove off. None of us spoke for about five miles. Then Bill said, 'Some people go looking for adventure.'

'Aye,' said Alan and I together. 'Some do.'

Our route took us away from the populous coastal plain of Northumberland and Durham. We turned inland towards the high hills of the Pennines, which we could now occasionally see rising clear and stately and unbelievably white before us. This was the backbone of England, and we would have to cross it. There was a chance that the roads would be impassable with snow, but there was an even greater chance that the main roads would be blocked by police. A quick telephone call to Bill's friend confirmed that the aunt was in rude health, so we took the High Road home.

As we climbed, the scenery changed from pits and plains to rolling fells and wide fertile dales. The world was pure with snow; all the man made sores were covered up, and the country shone in the pink whiteness of sun and snow. The roads were easily passable, and although driving was always a strain we had no worry that we would not get through.

We passed through West Auckland and Corbridge, both asleep in the Sabbath calm, then on to Hexham. Hexham, Haydon Bridge, Haltwhistle, we passed through them all, and at Greenhead began to descend the west slopes of the hills. We were now only thirty miles from Scotland, and I insisted on taking the wheel, for I was selfish enough to claim the honour of driving the Stone over the Border.

We came to Brampton. Still no sign of the police. We had not seen a police car for the last hundred miles. The next town was the border town of Longtown. At Longtown the road crosses the River Esk. Here, on the bridge, was the ideal place for a road block.

We grew tense and tenser. Bill rebuked me for speeding. I had unconsciously edged my foot down to shorten the suspense. My mouth was dry, and my stomach fluttered like a white flag in a storm.

'What do we do if there's a roadblock?' asked Alan.

'What can we do?' asked Bill.

'Toe down,' I said. It was only two miles from the bridge to Scotland. Roadblock or no roadblock, we would reach Scotland. Of that I was sure.

We came down the hill into Longtown. As we reached the bottom and turned the corner, a policeman disappeared into the door of the police station, leaving the street deserted.

'I hope that's symbolic,' whispered Bill. We turned another corner, and the long deserted length of the bridge was before us. I sighed.

'That's that,' said Bill.

Two miles further on at half past two in the afternoon we came to a sign that said SCOTLAND. We passed the sign and gave a little ragged cheer, and shook hands. We were most moved. Success is a strange thing, much nearer to tears than to laughter.

A handful of miles inside Scotland we stopped. The symbol of her liberty had come back to Scotland, and we felt that some sort of rude ceremony was needed to mark the return of the Lia Fail to the custody of its own people.

We stopped and drew the coat back and exposed the Stone to the air of Scotland for the first time in six hundred years. From the provision basket we produced the gill of whisky, and poured a libation over the Stone's roughness.

Thus, quietly, with little fuss, with no army, with no burning of houses or killing of people, and for the expenditure of less than a hundred pounds, we brought Scotland back the Stone of Destiny.

Forty years on

After all the excitement it was an anti climax, but there it was. I wish Johnny had been with us. It was miserable to send him off alone. I knew what the others did not know, that he suffered from a severe form of diabetes, which from time to time became uncontrollable, and which, one day soon, was to kill him. It had kept him from following the family career into the Royal Navy, although it was the Royal Marines he had wished to join. It never affected his love of life, which he lived to an over-brimming fullness. John's cup ever overflowed. He married very happily, emigrated to North America, and to my great grief, died a few years later, after fathering three children, one of whom has come back to live in Scotland. He was a strange, wild, brilliant character, and to this day I miss everything about him, especially his extremely phoney Scottish accent.

Chapter Twenty Six

Before we started off again, we spring cleaned the car, and satisfied ourselves that we had removed all evidence of our English trip. Our period of greatest danger had now passed, but there were still policemen in Scotland. They would be searching for the Stone, but they would not be searching so diligently. Indeed one nameless policeman had gone on record in one of the newspapers as saying, 'Aye! Sure we're looking for them, but no' so damned hard that we'll find them.' In England we were foreigners, and as Scots natural suspects. In Scotland we were at home, and any check on our identity and destination must only be a routine one.

We now determined that we were three members of the Students' Fifth Centenary Committee on our way back from a visit to Colonel Elliot, our newly retired Lord Rector. I had read that he was in London so it was unlikely that the police would check out our story. Bill and I were, in fact, members of that committee, and it was exactly the sort of story which might be true. We drove on in a daze through Dumfriesshire and Lanarkshire, our excitement over, our worry forgotten. We might indeed have been driving from a committee meeting, so simple our task seemed.

But another problem was looming up on the horizon and growing blacker like a fog cloud as we neared the city. When we had left Glasgow forty eight hours before, we had left with no definite plan in our minds. It had been an emergency action. We had been determined to get the Stone into safety before the frost did it any damage. We had succeeded in doing that, but now that we were approaching Glasgow we had no further idea of what to do, or where to go.

People who stand at the North Pole can go in only one direction. This is a very frustrating fact of life if you are of an independent cast of mind, and wish to exercise a personal choice. Yet sooner or later you realise that at the North Pole there is no personal choice.

You must move South, or be frozen. We found ourselves in that position. More correctly, I found myself in that position. This had all started as a child's dream of doing something for his country. The block of Stone upon which I was now sitting was only incidental to that dream; it was not an end in itself. Had it been an end in itself, I could have persuaded the other two to get out the car, then driven off and dumped the Stone somewhere it could never be found, and that would have been the end of it, Stone, problem, and all. It would have stayed in Scotland for ever, as part of the subsoil. That would have been no solution at all. The dream had been to wake Scotland up, and in that we had succeeded. It was the idea that mattered, not the corporeal thing. And the Stone was now very much a thing.

People who lack imagination see things only in physical terms. They do not speculate. They make statements. From that hour on we were showered with statements as to what we should do. Let anyone who cannot understand our problem read Mallory's stories about King Arthur and the Knights of the Round Table, or any other author's rehash of these old tales. Then let him ask the question, 'What do you do with the Holy Grail once you have found it?' If he can answer that question he has found the secret of the universe. Meanwhile I was sitting on the Holy Grail; Alan was driving, and Bill Craig was in the back seat fast asleep. Ahead of us were not the dreaming towers of Camelot, only a big city. I woke Bill up.

We discussed the matter for many miles. Alan wanted to take it home to Barrhead, but I would not hear of that. If he were arrested, as well he might be, the Stone would be taken too. Illogically I wanted to take it to my home in Perthshire, but that presented the same difficulty. Scotland was full of people who would have faced torture and death itself to keep the Stone. But secret custody was no answer. There is in the end no solution to the problem, which I now state. You cannot have private custody of a public symbol. The one negates the other.

All this talk occupied us until we neared Hamilton, and by that time we knew that there was no short term solution. The only thing we could do now was to get in touch with John MacCormick or Bertie Gray. At first we were against this idea. It was an age since we had left Glasgow, and anything might have happened. For all we knew they might be prime suspects, with their telephones tapped, and each with his private shadow. But that seemed a bit thick. The police would need to have some evidence before they could do such things to men as important as them. In any event, it was the best we could do. The Stone was becoming a millstone.

Near Bothwell we dropped Bill Craig. He was guest of honour at a Hogmanay party that night and had to go home and change. Alan and I drove on alone, less tired and more jaunty than the last time we had entered Glasgow by car, only four days previously. We drove along the Gallowgate just after darkness had fallen. The snow was churned and muddy, and had lost its beauty; the gas lamps gleamed wanly, and the old and crowded houses had an air of despair; but it was Glasgow. We were home again and proud to be citizens of no mean city. We went along Argyll Street and up Buchanan Street to Bath Street. At Pitt Street we turned down to the buildings of the telephone exchange, and while Alan sat on the Stone, I went into the telephone box and put through a call to Councillor Gray.

He was just sitting down to his dinner as I 'phoned but he left his soup to grow cold and came on immediately. I told him we would be waiting for him outside the King's Theatre.

I went back to Alan. We were both starving, and I remembered a little fish and chip shop in Great Western Road which kept open on a Sunday and which sold good fish and chips. We drove round to it and I got out and got two fish suppers, and then we drove back to the King's Theatre to await Councillor Gray. We sat eating our fish and chips out of their paper pokes, feeling the alternating sting of salt and vinegar at the corner of our mouths, and the bland taste of the fish on our tongues, and I was suddenly struck by the incongruity of it all. Alan's seat represented twenty centuries of known history, and I put my greasy hand under the old coat to

190

feel that it was real. It was. Outside the car, people went about their business. We were the centre of the biggest manhunt ever, yet our job was to sit casually in a busy street. Suddenly the delightful daftness of it all made me chuckle. I asked Alan for a wee shot on the Stone, and we swopped places. Then I went on eating my fish and chips.

We were wiping our greasy hands on the Stone of Destiny's royal tapestry when Bertie Gray arrived. At first he was all for solving the problem by hiding the Stone in his mason's yard which was only two hundred yards away, but I would not hear of it. Sooner or later the police would get round to visiting him, as indeed they did, only a few days later.

The Councillor paused for a moment to consider whom we could trust. They were many, but the person we were looking for must have attributes other than sheer trustworthiness. He must be discreet, and not given to boasting, for all over Scotland people were saying, 'I know where the Stone is hidden.' He must be of a like mind to us, for one day we would ask the Stone back from him when the time came to bring it to light. Above all he must be in a position to offer us a hiding place safe from weather and police alike. The Councillor left us to go round to his office to make a telephone call and park his car. In a few minutes he returned and got in beside us.

'Drive out towards Stirling,' he said. 'I've got the very man.'

As we drove, we asked no questions, but only answered his. He was thirsty for details of our weekend, and we told him all that had happened to us. At last he told us where we were going. After forty-five minutes driving we climbed a hill and came to a factory standing by itself in the darkness. Far in the distance shone the lights of a town. It was a lonely place, sad enough for an ending. We drove into the yard of the factory and our headlights swung round the grimy walls as we turned. A man was sitting in another car in the yard, and Councillor Gray got out and held a few minutes conversation with him in the darkness. The stranger disappeared, and shortly some lights came on inside the building.

The Taking of the Stone of Destiny

A great door opened and Alan drove carefully in. The door was shut behind us.

We found ourselves in a great, dim, silent barn, cumbered with massive machinery. Only a few lights were on, and the building seemed endless. The air smelt of oil and damp and iron filings. It was the kind of place which when silent seemed dead. Apart from the scrape of our feet and our whispered voices, all was hushed.

We were introduced to our custodian under false names. I pulled the coat back from the Stone, and he looked at it with silent concentration. Then he put his hand forward and reverently touched it.

'Guard it with your life.' I said. 'They may arrest us and hold us at the Court's discretion until it is produced, but no matter what happens, don't give it up.'

He said nothing, but only smiled grimly. I think he would have delighted in torture for the chance not to betray the Stone.

We lifted it from the car and lowered it into a packing case, and then we turned to leave and go back into the darkness again. As I went out, I took one last look at the Stone lying in the box like a common piece of masonry. It had grown to be part of my life, like a mother, or a lover, or a dear friend. Now I was to turn my back on it. My job was done and others were to take over where I had left off. I did not see the Stone again until we were on the way to Arbroath to lay it on the high altar of the ruined Abbey there.

All the way back to Glasgow I said little. Alan drove me to my lonely little room at the top of a tenement in Park Quadrant. Johnny had been there before us, for the car seat was lying under my bed. Alan pressed me to go with him to bring in the New Year with his family, but I wanted solitude and would not go. We said goodbye, and he went off to face his father. I've always thought the world of Alan.

In a short time Johnny came in. When he saw me and heard of our success, he was jubilant, and could not sit still for joy. I was strangely remote from him. He too wanted me to go to a party, but I could not face a crowd, and he departed reluctantly, knowing there was nothing he could do for me. I had lost contact with people.

I lay on my bed and smoked a cigarette, as I had lain on my bed so often before and planned and dreamed. All that was finished. We had succeeded.

Yet success was not enough. Success in the midst of strife, and achievement after struggle, are both unalloyed happiness; but final success is a finish, and no one likes to finish. It was a death.

For nine glorious days in the balance of decision and the cleanness of action I had carried responsibility. I had lived, not to eat or drink or strive after selfish ends, but to achieve. I had achieved, and now life had receded from me. I had handed over my charge to others. For nine days I had been the most privileged young man in the world. I had not only been able to make decisions, I had also been able to carry them through to their conclusion. Now the decisions to be taken were no longer mine, and anyone could carry them through. All was commonplace. I did not think it was worth wasting energy to live.

I fell asleep. Towards midnight I wakened up, and got up and took off my clothes and went back to bed. On a neighbour's wireless Big Ben beat in the New Year.

I awakened next morning sick at heart. Scotland was on the move again, yet there seemed to be no place for me. I had shot my bolt. I felt that at twenty five I had fulfilled all my ambitions. The world held nothing more that I wanted.

'If only the police would come,' I thought. I was ravenous for more excitement.

Suddenly there was a knocking at my door. Joy came surging over me from the fear of it.

'Who's there?' I called.

'It's the police,' came the quiet reply.

'Come in,' I cried. 'And welcome! I've been waiting for you.'

I was alive again.

The Taking of the Stone of Destiny

Forty years on

I still remember the desolation of that Hogmanay and that New Year's day. The policeman departed and left me alone, and although I had many friends to turn to, I was really lonely. It had taken nine days to fulfil a childhood ambition and I had thought that it would all be a nine days' wonder, and that after a spell in jail I would be able to get on with my life. The fact that you are reading about it forty years later shows that I was wrong. I had to rebuild my life to include the events of these nine days, and that was not easy. I have told the story elsewhere[1], but it started in loneliness that Hogmanay.

The man to whom we handed the Stone was John Rollo, and the factory was his factory of Rollo Lathes at Bonnybridge. He kept the Stone until the decision was taken to hand it back. Before he died he recorded a tape, explaining his part in the enterprise. He never liked me, which was a pity, because I always had a great affection and respect for him. Single-handed he had created the Highland Fund to enable youngsters to settle on crofts in the Highlands, and he built a small factory at Easdale to help unemployment there. He used to pilot his own aircraft into North Connel airstrip, where I was later to station my own aeroplane, and near which I now live. We would have had much in common, but I was an arrogant intolerant youngster, as these pages show, and there was much about me to dislike. It was my misfortune, but I have never looked over my shoulder to see what people are thinking, and I have paid the price for that characteristic. Friendship with John Rollo was part of that price, and I found it a hard one to pay.

Footnote.
[1] *A Touch of Treason*, Lochar 1990

Chapter Twenty Seven

That is the end of my personal story of the recovery of the Stone of Destiny. My part finished with the Stone lying in hiding in Scotland. It is true that I took part in all the discussions that followed, and homologated all the decisions that were made, but these were political decisions, and I am no politician. I regard the rest as anti-climax. A spectacular demonstration for my country, like sending flowers to a forlorn love, had been my intent, and I had done that. As far as I am concerned, the story ended at Bonnybridge. Yet, being party to the events which followed, I record them here.

These events are simple enough to narrate. The detective who called on me on New Year's Day was Calum Robertson, the Skyeman I have mentioned already, and he was soon satisfied that I was innocent, or so he said. I have always had my suspicion that that man of the old blood was not so easily deceived. Perhaps . . . perhaps . . . There were many people of divided loyalties over that affair, and not for the first time in Scotland either. In any event my alibi was checked out with my father, and I seemed to be free of suspicion. The following weekend, I took the train to Birmingham, and returned driving the Anglia, with Kay's smaller piece of the Stone.

Then followed a period of inactivity on our part. The problem of what to do with the Stone went unresolved. In retrospect it would have been better if we had been caught with it, somewhere in Scotland, and then the problem would have been the Government's, not ours. We were the victims of our own success. Public pressure mounted for its return. Not its return to England, but its return to some public place. I give one example of many. Sir John Cameron, the Dean of the Faculty of Advocates, called publicly for us to produce it, and then work openly for its retention in Scotland. We were in a quandary.

For this quandary there was no easy solution. We had caught

195

the imagination of the world, and the Scottish reaction can only be described as fervent, indeed almost awed, support. But support for what? Support for our actions certainly, but not support for the total disappearance for ever of the Stone. From time to time we sensed a shift in public opinion, and as the weeks went past, it seemed clear to us that public opinion wanted some end to the matter, but no end could be found to satisfy all parties. So far as I am aware, the Government resolutely refused to negotiate, while at the same time dropping hints that if it were returned openly, sympathetic consideration would be given to the Stone's retention in Scotland. While the Stone was at Westminster, the capital of the country, so one line of argument ran, the Scots knew where it was. Better there, than lost for ever. On the other hand, if we made a generous gesture, so might the other side, and some compromise could be reached.

Well, that was one view. It was not mine. If there was to be a compromise I wanted to know what it was. I did not, do not and never will trust an Englishman in political office. Nice people as they are, they carry power as badly as a Scot carries drink. I wanted to see the colour of their public promise, before I would even think of compromise. At one time I advocated sending a champed up piece of the Stone once a week to the Dean of Westminster as a heartener. Not much; just an ounce or two. I was wrong, of course. You can't champ up the talisman of your people. But something was needed to bring matters to a head. We attempted to do this by reiterating our aims in a further statement like our first petition. It was typed out on the same typewriter, and Kay and I travelled through to Edinburgh and nailed it to the west door of St Giles. The press loved it; the church organist who had been playing away alone inside was arrested; but the Government did not budge. Further factors began to point to the necessity for us to surrender it.

These factors can be summed up in two words, and these two words are 'common sense'. John MacCormick was a moderate, long-headed man, who knew every breath and shift of public opinion in Scotland. At that time there was no political movement of any significance in Scotland demanding separation, and the wartime frolics of a handful of extremists, whose slogan was 'Scotland free and neutral', had brought the whole Scottish movement into disrepute. But there was an enormous groundswell of support for devolution, whatever that might mean. John MacCormick, as the acknowledged leader of that movement, did not want to see it all break and come apart on this Stone which I had produced for him. He felt that that support was about to be alienated, and he came to me with these arguments.

We were, he said, four young people who had done a great thing for our country. To the original four, there had been added some others, and sooner or later the police would find us. Prosecutions would follow, and he and the rest of the Covenant leadership would be put in the position of seeing us prosecuted for an action to which they were a party. Nothing could more surely alienate public opinion than the suggestion that we were in the dock, only because behind us there were older men who held onto the Stone, and would not give it up even to save us from prison. Our martyrdom, if such it could be called, would be laid at the door not of the auld enemy, but attributed instead to the pointless stubborness of himself and Bertie Gray.

Young men with causes are keen to be martyrs, and I was no exception. Yet there were Kay and Alan and all the others to be considered, and I began to realise that things were no longer black or white, and that between them there were many different shades of grey representing different opinions. Whatever happened, I was then, and still am, a great admirer of John MacCormick. He was the founding father of the modern political movement in Scotland. He is Scotland's forgotten patriot. I listened to him, and saw the wisdom in what he said. I confess to a reluctance, but it was a selfish reluctance, because I saw myself in the dock in a righteous cause, and whatever happened thereafter would be a fitting end to the enterprise I had dreamed of since childhood.

Meanwhile, the police worked steadily away. We knew that arrest could not long be delayed. These were days of suppressed excitement, and for my part, fear never entered into the equation. I had done what I thought was right, and I had no hesitation in standing by what I had done, and indeed standing up for it. I was willing to pay any penalty, and I looked forward to finding a forum from which to restate my dream. A court is the best forum. We nearly reached that forum.

In the middle of March, to the great delight and animation of the Press, Detective Inspector McGrath of Scotland Yard came with an assistant to Scotland. They spent the first day interviewing peripheral suspects in Glasgow. Then they went north to Plockton, where Kay had recently taken up a teaching appointment. They questioned her alone, and with no friend to help or guide her, for five and a half hours, while the shadow of English chivalry yawned and wondered why the girl would not break down and confess.

Two days later they came for Alan and Gavin and me. It was no surprise, and I am glad to have experienced the early morning knock that is so dreaded in any country where the police have more power than is good for them, and us. At first I refused to go, as was my right. I handed Calum Robertson the standard work on the constitution, and told him to read it, much to his discomfiture. However, when I heard that Alan and Gavin were already in the police station, I went voluntarily. I enjoyed the interview with McGrath; made no admissions, and fenced with him politely. Behind me stood a ring of Glasgow policemen designed to intimidate me. McGrath was not the world's finest interviewer, and when I scored the odd point off him and heard from the Glasgow police behind me a cough which sounded oddly like a chuckle, it did much for my morale. It is an experience I would not have missed. Then they let us go.

This deepened all our problems. Hidden in a cellar the Stone was as valueless to us as it was to the Dean and Chapter of Westminster. We could see no solution, and to this day, and I write this paragraph forty years on, I still cannot see what could have been done. We had to produce the Stone before public opinion turned against us. This was a stark necessity. It appeared to us that by rounding off the incident in this way it could not but advance the political aspect of our cause. And so far as my own childhood dream of giving Scotland back her soul was concerned, I had done as much as I could. It was for the people themselves to go on now.

It was for these reasons that we put the ball back at the feet of the authorities. They could do two things. They could please the people of Scotland by leaving the Stone in Scotland, or they could please the English establishment by unceremoniously bundling it back over the Border. Unfortunately for everyone, Scots as well as English, they were incapable of the grand gesture. They chose the latter course. They swooped on the Stone in a panic. They locked it over-night in a police cell as though it had been common loot, and they sneaked it back over the Border at dead of night while a great roar of protest went up in Scotland.

As the place to return it, we chose the ruins of the great Abbey of Arbroath, where in 1320 the Arbroath Declaration had been signed by the Lords, Commons and Clergy of Scotland. In it they had reaffirmed our right to be free to live our own lives in our own way.

On the morning of 11 April 1951, I left Glasgow with Bill Craig. At Stirling Bridge we thumbed a lift from a car driven by Councillor Gray, which contained the Stone of Destiny, now carefully repaired. At midday we carried it down the grass-floored nave of the Abbey and left it at the High Altar. It was a crucifixion.

When we turned away and stood for a minute at the gate, and looked down the long nave flanked by the blood-red sandstone of the walls to the altar where the Stone lay under the blue and white of a Saltire, I heard the voice of Scotland speak as clearly as it spoke in 1320:

'For so long as one hundred of us remain alive we will yield in no least way to the domination of the English. We fight not for glory nor for wealth nor for honours, but only and alone for freedom, which no good man surrenders but with his life.'

I never saw the Stone again.

Forty years on

And to this day I have never seen the Stone again. I don't believe in looking back.

This last chapter was a sad one to write, and it recalled many unhappy memories. Of course we were bitterly criticised by many people for returning it. For years I had to endure the taunts of people that I had traded it for my freedom. I need hardly say that that is quite untrue, and that all my instincts called upon me to go through the dock to whatever might befall. I treated the jibes with uncharacteristic silence, yet to this day I have a haunting feeling that somehow I failed. The jibes did not help.

'If it had been me,' the jibes went, 'I would never have handed it back.'

I longed to seize such a commentator by the lapels, put the heid on him, and say, 'If it had been you, you bastard, it would never have been taken in the first place,' but I have suffered all those years in silence, turning away from the matter, and never discussing anything to do with the Stone. This chapter has helped to exorcise a ghost.

One thing more. It was the Stone which came from Westminster which went back. I am all sorts of a bastard, but I don't cheat. I and I alone took the responsibility to return the Stone. Not John MacCormick, not Bertie Gray, not John Rollo, nor any other of the loyal Scots who stood by me. It was left by them all to me to decide. It was I who took that decision. Myself alone. That decision marked me out as a lonely man for the rest of my life.

Epilogue

We were not prosecuted. A few weeks later the Home Secretary announced that it would not be in the public interest to prosecute us. He was right. Scottish public opinion was so outraged by the way the Stone had been rushed incontinently back to England that the ordinary people of this country might have risen in public disorder at our prosecution. In the course of his address to the House of Commons the Home Secretary referred to us as 'thieves and vulgar vandals.' Not one Scottish MP rose to our defence. No one cried out in our support.

I won fame and fortune from the Stone of Destiny. I hate fame. It gives everyone a licence to speak to you, and you are expected to be an instant raree show on their chosen subject. Press the button, and Ian Hamilton will talk about the Stone. I hated that. I clammed up. My friends know and respect my privacy. When others approach me, I endure.

As for the fortune, that came from selling the story to a Sunday newspaper. I would have none of it. I refused. Finally I agreed, on condition that I wrote the story for the Covenant Association, and they could do what they liked with it. I believe it went for a king's ransom. I don't know how much, and I never asked. It financed the Home Rule movement for some years. I have been in debt and in love and in trouble all the days of my life, but I am glad I never touched that money. I wrote a book about the event which had a modest success. I kept the royalties from the book, because they represented my labour in writing it, but it never made me rich.

As for the others, I have already written about my great friend Johnny Josselyn. Bill Craig went into industry. He is somewhere in Scotland, but we have drifted apart and I have not seen him for many years. Gavin is in America, doing very well. Alan went into the family business, and then branched out on his own, and has made a great success of his life. He lives in his own castle in the West of Scotland.

Kay did not lose her job after all. She returned to her beloved Gaelic people where she has remained to this day, quietly teaching and ever maintaining the rights of the Celtic people to their own way of life. She never married. I have not seen her for nearly forty years. I never look back. Yet I often wonder what she thinks of me and of these five days we spent together. She is beyond all my praise and understanding.

I turn now to myself. For some years after 1951 I stumped around Scotland addressing audiences in the Home Rule cause, for it was still the days of the public meeting and the public speech. I spoke in every town and village of any size in Scotland. I developed a facility for public speaking, but not for politics, and gradually I withdrew from public life. It is not a choice I have regretted. I am not a committee man, and public life in a democracy is one of committee meetings. I have gone my own private way.

I married the girl from Sunderland. We had three children, and after eleven tempestuous years we separated. The children are still my friends, and so, for that matter, is she. There was another short marriage, and then I was on my own again. In my late forties I was making a solo trip across Scotland by slalom canoe, ever an exciting experience, when I had to swim for it in the torrent of tidal waters known as the Falls of Lora where Loch Etive meets the sea. I met Jeannette on the shore and we were married a year later. That was a long time ago. She has taught me gentleness, a lesson at which I was never an apt pupil, and against which teaching I sometimes rebel. We have one son, Stewart.

When Stewart was nine years old Jeannette took him to Westminster Abbey to see the Stone of Destiny. It is now kept behind bars. Somewhere perhaps, there dreams another schoolboy, as I dreamed all these years ago. Although Stewart reached through the bars he could not touch the talisman of his own people. The lesson was not lost on him. It should not be lost on any Scot.

The question remains, was it worth the trouble? Was it worth changing my life for such a gesture? To that question I make this answer. History is ideas. Deeds are only the manifestation of ideas. We made manifest an idea. Nobody sang in Scotland in the middle part of this century. To be more correct, those who sang did not derive their songs from Scotland. Their sources were foreign and what they sang was only an alien copy of other peoples' ways of life. Now everyone sings Scottish songs, and if I were a unionist politician of whatever party, but especially of the Labour Party, I would be counting the songs, rather than the votes. The people who make the songs of a country, have a habit of making the laws also.

When, on 25 March 1707, James Ogilvie, Earl of Seafield, Chancellor of Scotland, signed the Act of Union, ending Scotland's ancient independence, and merging the two Parliaments of Scotland and England into the United Kingdom Parliament, he threw down the quill with these words, 'Now there's the end of an auld sang.'

It may be, it just may be, that on Christmas Day 1950 four young people wrote a new verse to that old song. Whatever we did, the song is still being sung.